The Mind of Primitive Man

By

Franz Boas

Published by Forgotten Books 2012

Originally Published 1922

PIBN 1000060486

THE MIND OF PRIMITIVE MAN

THE MACMILLAN COMPANY
NEW YORK · BOSTON · CHICAGO
SAN FRANCISCO

MACMILLAN & CO., LIMITED
LONDON · BOMBAY · CALCUTTA
MELBOURNE

THE MACMILLAN CO. OF CANADA, LTD.
TORONTO

THE

MIND OF PRIMITIVE MAN

BY

FRANZ BOAS

A COURSE OF LECTURES DELIVERED BEFORE THE LOWELL
INSTITUTE, BOSTON, MASS., AND THE NATIONAL
UNIVERSITY OF MEXICO, 1910–1911

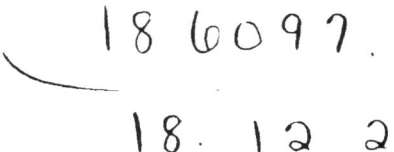

New York

THE MACMILLAN COMPANY

1922

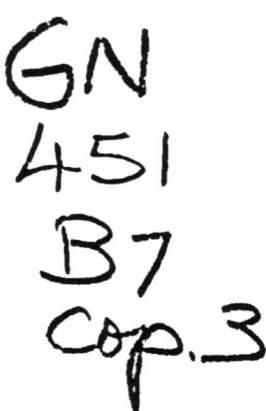

Norwood Press
J. S. Cushing Co. — Berwick & Smith Co.
Norwood, Mass., U.S.A.

PREFACE

THE problem discussed in the following pages has occupied my attention for many years, and I have at various times dealt with it in brief essays. Some of these, in revised form and enlarged, are embodied in the present volume : —

Human Faculty as determined by Race (*Proceedings of the American Association for the Advancement of Science*, vol. xliii [1894], pp. 301–327).

The Limitations of the Comparative Method of Anthropology (*Science*, N. S., vol. iv [1896], pp. 901–908).

The Mind of Primitive Man (*Journal of American Folk-Lore*, vol. xiv [1901], pp. 1–11).

Some Traits of Primitive Culture (*Ibid.*, vol. xvii [1904], pp. 243–254).

Race Problems in America (*Science*, N. S., vol. xxix [1909], pp. 839–849).

Psychological Problems in Anthropology (*American Journal of Psychology*, vol. xxi [1910], pp. 371–384).

I have also utilized a small part of the Introduction to my "Handbook of American Indian Languages"

(Bulletin 40 of the Bureau of American Ethnology), and some of the results of my report on " Changes in Bodily Form of Descendants of Immigrants " (vol. 39, Reports of the Immigration Commission, Washington, Government Printing Office).

FRANZ BOAS.

CONTENTS

THE MIND OF PRIMITIVE MAN

THE MIND OF PRIMITIVE MAN

I. RACIAL PREJUDICES

PROUD of his wonderful achievements, civilized man looks down upon the humbler members of mankind. He has conquered the forces of nature and compelled them to serve him. He has transformed inhospitable forests into fertile fields. The mountain fastnesses are yielding their treasures to his demands. The fierce animals which are obstructing his progress are being exterminated, while others which are useful to him are made to increase a thousand-fold. The waves of the ocean carry him from land to land, and towering mountain-ranges set him no bounds. His genius has moulded inert matter into powerful machines which await a touch of his hand to serve his manifold demands.

With pity he looks down upon those members of the human race who have not succeeded in subduing nature; who labor to eke a meagre existence out of the products of the wilderness; who hear with trembling the roar of the wild animals, and see the products of their toils destroyed by them; who remain restricted by ocean, river, or mountains; who strive to obtain the necessities of life with the help of few and simple instruments.

Such is the contrast that presents itself to the observer. What wonder if civilized man considers himself a being of higher order as compared to primitive man, if he claims that the white race represents a type higher than all others!

Before accepting this conclusion which places the stamp of eternal inferiority upon whole races of man, we may well pause, and subject the basis of our opinions regarding the aptitude of different peoples and races to a searching analysis. The naïve assumption of the superiority of the European nations and their descendants is obviously based upon their wonderful achievements. We conclude that, as the civilization is higher, the aptitude for civilization is also higher; and, as the aptitude for civilization presumably depends upon the perfection of the mechanism of body and mind, the inference is drawn that the white race represents the highest type of perfection. In this conclusion, which is reached through a comparison of the social status of civilized man with that of primitive man, the tacit assumption is made that achievement depends solely, or at least primarily, upon the aptitude for an achievement.

The assertion of a higher aptitude of the European nations leads at once to a second inference relating to the significance of difference in type between the European race and the races of other continents, or even of differences between various European types. The line of thought which we unconsciously pursue is about as follows. Since the aptitude of the European is highest, his physical and mental type is also highest, and every deviation from the white type necessarily represents a characteristic feature of a lower type.

That this unproved assumption underlies our judgments of races, appears from the fact, that, other conditions being equal, a race is commonly described as the lower, the more fundamentally it differs from the white race. Its effect may also be noticed in the long-continued discussions of the occurrence of anatomical peculiarities in primitive man which would characterize him as a being of lower order in the zoological series, and in the emphasis laid upon the non-occurrence of such traits in primitive man and their occurrence in the European race.

The subject and form of these discussions show that

the idea dwells in the minds of investigators that we should expect to find in the white race the highest type of man.

In drawing inferences from social distinctions, the same point of view is frequently held. It is assumed, that, as the mental development of the white race is the highest, it also has the highest aptitude in this direction, and therefore its mind is supposed to have the most subtile organization. As the ultimate psychical causes are not so apparent as anatomical characteristics, the judgment of the mental status of a people is generally guided by the difference between its social status and our own : the greater the difference between their intellectual, emotional, and moral processes and those which are found in our civilization, the harsher the judgment on the people. It is only when a Tacitus finds the virtues of past stages of the life of his own people among foreign tribes that their example is held up to the gaze of his fellow-citizens, who probably had a pitying smile for the dreamer who clung to the ideas of a time which they had left far behind.

In order to understand clearly the relations between race and civilization, the two unproved assumptions to which I have referred must be subjected to a searching analysis. We must investigate in how far we are justified in assuming that achievement is primarily due to exceptional aptitude, and in how far we are justified in assuming that the European type — or, taking the notion in its extreme form, that the North European type – represents the highest development of mankind. It will be advantageous to clear up these points before we take up the detailed inquiry.

In regard to the former point, it might be said, that, although achievement is not necessarily a measure of aptitude, it seems admissible to judge the one by the other. Have not most races had the same chances for development? Why, then, did the white race alone develop a civilization which is sweeping the whole world, and compared to which all other civilizations appear as feeble beginnings cut short in early childhood, or arrested and petrified in an early stage of development? Is it not, to say the least, probable that the race which attained the highest stage of civilization was the most gifted one, and that those races which remained at the bottom of the scale were not capable of rising to higher levels?

In order to find an answer to these questions, let us consider briefly the general outlines of the history of civilization; let our minds go back a few thousand years, until we reach the time when the civilizations of eastern and of western Asia were in their infancy. As time passed on, these civilizations were transferred from one people to another; some of those who had represented the highest type of culture sinking back into obscurity, while others took their places. During the dawn of history we see civilization cling to certain districts, in which it is taken up, now by one people, now by another. In the numerous conflicts of these times the more civilized people were often vanquished. The conqueror, however, learned the arts of life from the conquered, and carried on the work of civilization. Thus the centres of civilization were shifting to and fro over a limited area, and progress was slow and halting. At the same period the ancestors of the races that are now among the most highly civilized were in no way superior to primitive man as we find him now in regions that have not come into contact with modern civilization.

Was the civilization attained by these ancient people of such character as to allow us to claim for them a genius superior to that of any other race ?

First of all, we must bear in mind that none of these

civilizations was the product of the genius of a single people. Ideas and inventions were carried from one to the other; and, although intercommunication was slow, each people which participated in the ancient development contributed its share to the general progress. Proofs without number have been forthcoming which show that ideas have been disseminated as long as people have come into contact with one another, and that neither race nor language nor distance limits their diffusion. As all have worked together in the development of the ancient civilizations, we must bow to the genius of all, whatever group of mankind they may represent, — Hamitic, Semitic, Aryan, or Mongol.

We may now ask, Did no other races develop a culture of equal value? It would seem that the civilizations of ancient Peru and of Central America may well be compared with the ancient civilizations of the Old World. In both we find a high stage of political organization : we find division of labor and an elaborate ecclesiastical organization. Great architectural works were undertaken, requiring the co-operation of many individuals. Animals and plants were domesticated, and the art of writing had been invented. The inventions and knowledge of the peoples of the Old World seem to have been somewhat

more numerous and extended than those of the races of
the New World, but there can be no doubt that the
general status of their civilization was nearly equally
high.[1]   This will suffice for our consideration.

What, then, is the difference between the civilization
of the Old World and that of the New World? It is
essentially a difference in time.   The one reached a certain stage three thousand or four thousand years sooner
than the other.

Although much stress has been laid upon this greater
rapidity of development in the Old World, I think that it
is not by any means proof of greater ability of the races
of the Old World, but that it is adequately explained by
the laws of chance.   When two bodies run through the
same course with variable rapidity, sometimes quickly,
sometimes slowly, their relative position will be more
likely to show accidental differences, the longer the course
which they run.   Thus two infants a few months old will
be much alike in their physiological and psychical development; two youths of equal age will differ much more;
and two old men of equal age may, the one still be in full
possession of his powers, the other on the decline, due
mainly to the accidental acceleration or retardation of

[1] For authorities, see note to this page at end of book.

their development. The difference in period of development does not signify that the one is by heredity structurally inferior to the others.

Applying the same reasoning to the history of mankind, we may say that the difference of a few thousand years is insignificant as compared to the age of the human race. The time required to develop the existing races is entirely a matter of conjecture, but we may be sure that it is long. We also know that man existed in the Eastern and Western Hemispheres at a time that can be measured by geological standards only. Penck's recent investigations on the glacial age in the Alps have led him to the conclusion that the age of man must be measured by a span of time exceeding one hundred thousand years, and that the highly specialized civilization of the Magdalenian is not less than twenty thousand years old. There is no reason to believe that this stage was reached by mankind the world over at the same period, but we must assume as the initial point the remotest times in which we find traces of man. What does it mean, then, if one group of mankind reached the same stage at the age of a hundred thousand years as was reached by the other at the age of a hundred and four thousand years ? Would not the life-history of the people, and the vicissitudes of its history, be fully sufficient to explain a delay of this character, without necessitating us to assume a difference in their aptitude to social development? (See Waitz.) This retardation would be significant only if it could be shown that it occurs independently over and over again in the same race, while in other races greater rapidity of development was found repeatedly in independent cases.

The fact deserves attention, however, that at present practically all the members of the white race participate to a greater or less degree in the advance of civilization, while in none of the other races has the civilization that has been attained at one time or another been able to reach all the tribes or peoples of the same race. This does not necessarily mean that all the members of the white race had the power of originating and developing the germs of civilization with equal rapidity; for there is no evidence that the cognate tribes which have all developed under the influence of a civilization originated by a few members of the race, would not, without this help, have required a much longer time to reach the high level which they now occupy. It seems to show, however, a remarkable power of assimilation, which has not manifested itself to an equal degree in any other race.

Thus the problem presents itself of discovering the

reason why the tribes of ancient Europe readily assimilated the civilization that was offered to them, while at
present we see primitive people dwindle away and become
degraded before the approach of civilization, instead of
being elevated by it.   Is not this a proof of a higher organization of the inhabitants of Europe?

I believe the reasons for this fact are not far to seek, and
do not necessarily lie in a greater ability of the races of
Europe and Asia.   First of all, in appearance these people
were alike to civilized man of their times.   Therefore
the fundamental difficulty for the rise of primitive people
— namely, that an individual who has risen to the level
of the higher civilization is still looked upon as belonging
to an inferior race — did not prevail.   Thus it was possible that in the colonies of ancient times society could
grow by accretion from among the more primitive people.

Furthermore, the devastating influences of diseases
which nowadays begin to ravage the inhabitants of territories newly opened to the whites were not so strong, on
account of the permanent contiguity of the people of the
Old World, who were always in contact with one another,
and therefore subject to the same influences.   The in-
vasion of America and Polynesia, on the other hand, was
accompanied by the introduction of new diseases among

the natives of these countries. The suffering and devastation wrought by epidemics which followed the discovery are too well known to be described in full. In all cases in which a material reduction in numbers occurs in a thinly settled area, the economic life, as well as the social structure, is almost completely destroyed.

In addition to this, it may be said that the contrast between the culture represented by the modern white and that of primitive man is far more fundamental than that between the ancients and the people with whom they came in contact. Particularly, the methods of manufacture have developed so enormously, that the industries of the primitive people of our times are exterminated by the cheapness and large quantity of the products imported by the white trader, because primitive man is unable to compete with the power of production of the machines of the whites, while in olden times the superior hand-product rivalled the hand-product of a lower type. When a day's work suffices for obtaining efficient tools or fabrics from the trader, while the manufacture of the corresponding implement or material by the native himself would have required weeks, it is but natural that the slower and more laborious process should be given up speedily. It must also be considered that in several regions, particularly in America and in parts of Siberia, the primitive tribes are swamped by the numbers of the immigrating race, which is crowding them so rapidly out of their old haunts that no time for gradual assimilation is given. In olden times there was certainly no such immense inequality in numbers as we observe in many regions nowadays.

We conclude, therefore, that the conditions for assimilation in ancient Europe were much more favorable than in those countries where in our times primitive people come into contact with civilization. Therefore we do not need to assume that the ancient Europeans were more gifted than other races which have not become exposed to the influences of civilization until recent times (Gerland, Ratzel).

This conclusion may be corroborated by other facts. In the middle ages the civilization of the Arabs had reached a stage which was undoubtedly superior to that of many European nations of that period. Both civilizations had sprung largely from the same sources, and must be considered branches of one tree. The Arabs who were the carriers of civilization were by no means members of the same race as the Europeans, but nobody will dispute their high merits. It is of interest to see in what manner they influenced the negro races of the Soudan. At an early time, principally between the second half of the eighth century and the eleventh century of our era, the Soudan was invaded by Hamitic tribes, and Mohammedanism was spreading rapidly through the Sahara and the western Soudan. We see that since that time large empires have been formed, and have disappeared again in struggles with neighboring states, and that a relatively high degree of culture has been attained. The invaders intermarried with the natives; and the mixed races, some of which are almost purely negro, have risen high above the level of other African negroes. The history of Bornu is perhaps one of the best examples of this kind. Barth and Nachtigal have made us acquainted with the history of this state, which has played a most important part in the history of North Africa.

Why, then, have the Mohammedans been able to civilize these tribes, and to raise them to nearly the same standard which they had attained, while the whites have not been capable of influencing the negro in Africa to any considerable extent? Evidently on account of the different method of introduction of culture. While the Mohammedans influence the people in the same manner in which the ancients civilized the tribes of Europe, the whites send only the products of their manufactures and a few of their representatives into the negro country. A real amalgamation between the more highly educated whites and the negroes has never taken place. The amalgamation of the negroes by the Mohammedans is facilitated particularly by the institution of polygamy, the conquerors taking native wives, and raising their children as members of their own family.

The spread of the Chinese civilization in eastern Asia may be likened to that of the ancient civilization in Europe. Colonization and amalgamation of kindred tribes, and in some cases extermination of rebellious subjects, with subsequent colonization, have led to a remarkable uniformity of culture over a large area.

When, finally, we consider the inferior position held by the negro race of the United States, although the negro lives in the closest contact with modern civilization, we must not forget that the old race feeling of the inferiority of the colored race is as potent as ever, and is a formidable obstacle to its advance and progress, notwithstanding that schools and universities are open to them. We might rather wonder how much has been accomplished in a short period against heavy odds. It is hardly possible to say what would become of the negro if he were able to live with the whites on absolutely equal terms. Miss Ovington's discussion of the opportunities of the negro in the United States is a convincing proof of the inequality of the conditions of economic advance of the negro and of the white, even after the abolition of legal inequality.

Our conclusion drawn from the foregoing considerations is the following: Several races have developed a civilization of a type similar to the one from which our own had its origin. A number of favorable conditions facilitated the rapid spread of this civilization in Europe. Among these, common physical appearance, contiguity of habitat, and moderate difference in modes of manufacture, were the most potent. When, later on, civilization began to spread over other continents, the races with which modern civilization came into contact were not equally favorably situated. Striking differences of racial types, the preceding isolation which caused devastating epidemics in the newly discovered countries, and the greater advance in civilization, made assimilation much more difficult. The rapid dissemination of Europeans over the whole world destroyed all promising beginnings which had arisen in various regions. Thus no race except that of eastern Asia was given a chance to develop an independent civilization. The spread of the European race cut short the growth of the existing independent germs without regard to the mental aptitude of the people among whom it was developing. On the other hand, we have seen that no great weight can be attributed to the earlier rise of civilization in the Old World, which is satisfactorily explained as a chance. In short, historical events appear to have been much more potent in leading races to civilization than their faculty, and it follows that achievements of races do not warrant us in assuming that one race is more highly gifted than the other.

After having thus found an answer to our first problem, we turn to the second one : In how far are we justified in considering those anatomical traits in regard to which foreign races differ from the white race as marks of inferiority ? In one respect the answer to this question is easier than that to the former. We have recognized that achievement alone does not justify us in assuming greater mental ability for the white race than for others, unless we can sustain our claim by other proofs. It follows from this, that differences between the white race and other races must not be interpreted to mean superiority of the former, inferiority of the latter, unless this relation can be proved by anatomical or physiological considerations.

It may not be amiss to illustrate by an example the logical error which is committed with great ease and great frequency. In a painstaking investigation made a few years ago, Mr. R. B. Bean demonstrated certain characteristic differences between the form of the whole and of the parts of the brain of the Baltimore negro and of the Baltimore white, — differences which consist in the form and relative size of the frontal and occipital lobes and in the size of the *corpus callosum*. The interpretation of the difference is, that the smaller size of the anterior lobes and of the *callosum* indicates a lower mental development, a conclusion which has been refuted by Franklin P. Mall. It may suffice here, where we are interested chiefly in the logical fallacy of such conclusions, to call attention to the fact that a comparison of long-headed and short-headed individuals of the same race — or, let us say, of long-headed North French and of short-headed Central French — would result in similar differences, but that in a case of this kind the inference regarding greater or lesser ability would not be made with the same readiness.

There is, of course, no doubt that great differences exist in the physical characteristics of the races of man. The color of the skin, the form of the hair, and the configuration of lips and nose, distinguish the African clearly from the European. The question to decide is, What relations have these features to the mental aptitude of a race? Two points of view may be brought forward in relation to this question. First, we may claim that a race in which peculiarities are found that are characteristic of lower stages in the animal series will be in all respects of an inferior type. Secondly, we may direct our attention primarily to the central nervous sytem, and investigate whether the anatomical structure in one race is superior to that found in another race.

To illustrate the former viewpoint, I will mention a few of the formations in man which have been described as characterizing lower races, because they are found as typical developments in animals. One of these is a variation in the form of the temporal bone, which in man is ordinarily separated from the frontal bone by the sphenoid and parietal bones. It has been found that in some individuals the temporal bone encroaches upon the sphenoid and parietal, and comes into contact with the frontal bone. This formation is the prevalent one among the apes. It has been proved that this variation is found among all races, but with unequal frequency.

The peculiar formation of the tibia known as platycnemism (lateral flatness) has been observed in skeletons of the oldest remains of man in Europe, and also in the skeletons of various races. Other characteristics which remind us of lower forms are peculiarities in the formation of the articular surfaces of tibia and femur, which have been found in a number of human types; the *os Incæ*, or interparietal bone, which occurs among all races, but most frequently among the Peruvians and the inhabitants of the ancient pueblos; the smallness of the nasal bones and their synostosis with the maxilla; the so-called pre-nasal fossæ; and certain variations in the arrangement of arteries and of muscles. All these variable features are found among all races, but the degree of variability is not everywhere the same. Presumably such variations may be considered human characteristics which have not yet had time to become stable, and which in this sense may be considered as still in process of evolution. If this interpretation be correct, it might seem that we can consider those races in which the characteristic human features are more stable as those which are more highly organized.

It is also possible to arrange the races according to various typical features in such a manner that one appears farthest removed from the types of higher animals, others less so. In all these arrangements the gap be-- tween man and animal is a wide one, and the variations between the races are slight as compared to it. Thus we find, that, in comparison to the skull, the face of the negro is larger than that of the American, whose face is, in turn, larger than that of the white. The lower portion of his face has larger dimensions. The alveolar arch is pushed forward, and thus gains an appearance which re- minds us of the higher apes. There is no denying that this feature is a most constant character of the black races, and that it represents a type slightly nearer the animal than the European type. The same may be said of the broadness and flatness of the noses of the negro and the Mongol.

If we accept the general theories of Klaatsch, Stratz, and Schoetensack, who consider the Australian as the oldest and most generalized type of man, we might also call attention to the slenderness of the vertebræ, the un- developed curvature of the vertebral column, to which Cunningham first called attention, and the traits of the foot, which recall the needs of an animal living in trees, and whose feet had to serve the purpose of climbing from branch to branch.

In relation to the interpretation of all these observations, it must be strongly emphasized that the races which we are accustomed to call "higher races" do not by any means stand in all respects at the end of the series, and are farthest removed from the animal. The European and the Mongol have the largest brains; the European has a small face and a high nose; — all features farther removed from the probable animal ancestor of man than the corresponding features of other races. On the other hand, the European shares lower characteristics with the Australian, both retaining in the strongest degree the hairiness of the animal ancestor, while the specifically human development of the red lip is developed most markedly in the negro. The proportions of the limbs of the negro are also more markedly distinct from the corresponding proportions in the higher apes than are those of the European.

When we interpret these data in the light of modern biological concepts, we may say that the specifically human features appear with varying intensity in various races, and that the divergence from the animal ancestor has developed in varying directions.

When all these differences between races are given, the question arises, whether they have any significance in regard to mental faculty. I may be permitted to disregard for the moment differences in the size and structural development of the nervous system, and confine myself to the mental significance of other traits. The general analogy of mental development of animals and of man prompts us to associate lower mental traits with theromorphic features. In our naïve, every-day parlance, brutish features and brutality are closely connected. We must distinguish here, however, between the anatomical characteristics of which we have been speaking and the muscular development of the face, trunk, and limbs, due to habitual activity. The hand, which is never employed in activities requiring those refined adjustments which are characteristic of psychologically complex actions, will lack the modelling brought about by the development of each muscle. The face whose muscles have not responded to the innervations accompanying deep thought and refined sentiment will lack in individuality and refinement. The neck that has supported heavy loads, and has not responded to the varied requirements of delicate changes of position of head and body, will appear massive and clumsy. These physiognomic differences must not mislead us in our interpretations. But even without them, we are inclined to draw inferences in regard to mentality from a receding forehead, a heavy jaw, large and heavy teeth, perhaps even from an inordinate length of arms or an unusual development of hairiness.

From a strictly scientific point of view, these inferences seem to be open to the most serious doubt. Only a few investigations have been made in relation to these problems, but their results have been entirely negative. Most important among them is the elaborate attempt made by Karl Pearson to investigate the relationship of intelligence to size and shape of the head. His conclusions are so significant that I will repeat them here: "The onus of proof that other measurements and more subtle psychological observations would lead to more definite results may now, I think, be left to those who *a priori* regard such an association as probable. Personally, the result of the present inquiry has convinced me that there is little relationship between the external physical and the psychical character in man." I think all the investigations that have been made up to the present time compel us to assume that the characteristics of the osseous, muscular, visceral, or circulatory system, have practically no direct relation to the mental ability of man (Manouvrier).

We will now turn to the important subject of the size of the brain, which seems to be the one anatomical feature which bears directly upon the question at issue. It seems plausible that the greater the central nervous system, the higher the faculty of the race, and the greater its aptitude to mental achievements. Let us review the known facts. Two methods are open for ascertaining the size of the central nervous system, — the determination of the weight of the brain and that of the capacity of the cranial cavity. The first of these methods is the one which promises the most accurate results. Naturally, the number of Europeans whose brain-weights have been taken is much larger than that of individuals of other races. There are, however, sufficient data available to establish beyond a doubt the fact that the brain-weight of the whites is larger than that of most other races, particularly larger than that of the negroes. That of the white male is about 1360 grams. The investigations of cranial capacities are quite in accord with these results. According to Topinard, the capacity of the skull of males of the neolithic period in Europe is about 1560 cc. (44 cases) ; that of modern Europeans is the same (347 cases) ; of the Mongoloid race, 1510 cc. (68 cases) ; of African negroes, 1405 cc. (83 cases) ; and of negroes of the Pacific Ocean, 1460 cc. (46 cases). Here we have, therefore, a decided difference in favor of the white race.

In interpreting these facts, we must ask, Does the increase in the size of the brain prove an increase in faculty? This would seem highly probable, and facts may be adduced which speak in favor of this assumption. First among these is the relatively large size of the brain among the higher animals, and the still larger size in man. Furthermore, Manouvrier has measured the capacity of the skulls of thirty-five eminent men. He found that they averaged 1665 cc. as compared to 1560 cc. general average, which was derived from 110 individuals. On the other hand, he found that the cranial capacity of forty-five murderers was 1580 cc., also superior to the general average. The same result has been obtained through weighings of brains of eminent men. The brains of thirty-four of these showed an average increase of 93 grams over the average brain-weight of 1357 grams. Another fact which may be adduced in favor of the theory that greater brains are accompanied by higher faculty is that the heads of the best English students are larger than those of the average class of students (Galton). The force of the arguments furnished by these observations must, however, not be overestimated.

First of all, the brains of not all eminent men are unusually large. On the contrary, a few unusually small brains have been found in the series. Furthermore, most of the brain-weights constituting the general series are obtained in anatomical institutes; and the individuals who find their way there are poorly developed, on account of malnutrition and of life under unfavorable circumstances, while the eminent men represent a much better nourished class. As poor nourishment reduces the weight and size of the whole body, it will also reduce the size and weight of the brain. It is not certain, therefore, that the observed difference is entirely due to the higher ability of the eminent men. This may also explain the larger size of the brains of the professional classes as compared to those of unskilled laborers (Ferraira). An additional number of restricting facts must be enumerated. The most important among these is the difference in brain-weight between men and women. When men and women of the same stature are compared, it is found that the brain of woman is much lighter than that of man. Nevertheless the faculty of woman while perhaps qualitatively different from that of man, cannot be deemed to be of an inferior character. This is therefore a case in which smaller brain-weight is accompanied throughout by equal faculty. We conclude from this fact that it is not impossible that the smaller brains of males of other races should do the same work as is done by the larger brain of the white race. But this comparison is not quite on equal terms, as we may assume that there is a certain structural difference between male and female, which causes the difference in size between the sexes; so that comparison between male and female is not the same as comparison between male and male.

Notwithstanding these restrictions, the increase of the size of the brain in the higher animals, and the lack of development in microcephalic individuals, are fundamental facts which make it more than probable that increased size of the brain causes increased faculty, although the relation is not quite as immediate as is often assumed.

The reason for a lack of close correlation between brain-weight and mental faculties is not far to seek. The functioning of the brain depends upon the nerve cells and fibres, which do not constitute, by any means, the whole mass of the brain. A brain with many cells and complex connections between the cells may contain less connective tissue than another one of simpler nervous structure. In other words, if there is a close relation between form and ability, it must be looked for rather in the morphological traits of the brain than in its size. A correlation exists between size of brain and number of cells and fibres, but the correlation is weak (Donaldson).

Notwithstanding the numerous attempts that have been made to find structural differences between the brains of different races of man that could be directly interpreted in psychological terms, no conclusive results of any kind have been attained. The status of our present knowledge has been well summed up by Franklin P. Mall, to whose investigation I referred before. He holds, that, on account of the great variability of the individuals constituting each race, racial differences are exceedingly difficult to discover, and that up to the present time none have been found that will endure serious criticism.

We may now sum up the results of our preliminary inquiry. We have found that the unproved assumption of identity of cultural achievement and of mental ability is founded on an error of judgment; that the variations in cultural development can as well be explained by a consideration of the general course of historical events without recourse to the theory of material differences of mental faculty in different races. We have found, furthermore, that a similar error underlies the common assumption that the white race represents physically the highest type of man, but that anatomical and physiological considerations do not support these views.

II. INFLUENCE OF ENVIRONMENT UPON HUMAN TYPES

AFTER having seen that the high estimate of our civilization does not necessarily imply that the carriers of this
civilization have an anatomical organization superior to
that of all other races, we may turn our attention to a
closer investigation of the characteristics of different
divisions of mankind. It is clear that our investigations
cannot be based on vague descriptions of travellers, —
who remark upon the enormous digestive organs of primitive man, or on his small size, or on the lack of development of his limbs, or even upon his resemblance to apes,—
but on serious studies of anatomical characteristics.

Two problems may be distinguished here which have
too often been confounded in discussions of the mental
characteristics of civilized man and of primitive man.
The one relates to the distinctions between races; the
other, to distinctions between the social strata of the same
race. According to the meaning of the terms "civilized"
and "primitive," it is perfectly conceivable that there

may be civilized groups belonging to different races (like the Chinese and Europeans), and civilized as well as primitive groups, both belonging to the same race (like the Yukaghir of Siberia and the Chinese, or like the group of educated negroes in the United States and the primitive tribes of the coasts of Africa). The problems presented by the differences between the various races of man, and by the differences between social groups in the same races, are, of course, entirely distinct, and each requires separate treatment.

There is one peculiarity common to both problems, which must be described before we can properly take up their treatment. When we compare the individuals comprising any one racial or social type, we find that they are not by any means uniform, but exhibit considerable variation. When we try to think of a Norwegian and of a negro, two entirely distinct types will be present to our minds, — the Norwegian, tall, with blond and somewhat wavy hair, blue eyes, light complexion, delicate face and nose; the negro, of medium stature, with black and frizzly hair, dark eyes, dark skin, projecting jaw, and heavy flat nose. Still, these pictures are only abstractions of what we think we have noticed most commonly in each type. When we compare the Norwegians among themselves, or the negroes among themselves, we find that each individual in each series has his peculiarities, which the others do not share.   There are tall and short Norwegians; their hair is blond or dark, straight or wavy; their eyes vary from brown to blue; their complexion is light or dark, their faces more or less delicate.   And so with the negroes.   The degree of blackness, the amount of projection of the chin, the flatness of the nose, — all show very considerable variations.   Experience has demonstrated that in all cases of this kind, one certain type, one certain combination of features, is most common; and that deviations in either direction from this type become the rarer, the greater their amount.   Thus the Norwegians show a prevalence of a certain blond color.   Individuals with a color of hair much lighter than the most common color are the rarer, the greater the difference of their hair-color from the most common one; and in the same way individuals with a color of hair much darker than the most common color are the rarer, the greater the deviation of their color of hair from the common one.   The extent to which such variations occur is not always the same.   In some cases the individuals constituting the group show a remarkable similarity or uniformity of type; in other cases the diversity of types occurring in the same community is quite remarkable. We call a series the more variable, the more frequently deviating types occur in it; so that the average amount of differences between the individuals constituting the series and the most common type may be used as a measure of the variability of the series.

These considerations are of prime importance in all attempts to compare different races. In some cases differences are found which are sufficiently fundamental to distinguish easily and definitely one from another. Thus the color of the skin, color and form of the hair, and configuration of lips and nose, distinguish the African negro definitely from the North European. When, however, we compare all the races and types of man, we find that innumerable transitions exist, which would make it difficult to state that any one particular feature belongs to all the individuals of one type, to the exclusion of all others. Thus it would not be difficult to find among members of the American race, for instance, lips and nose which approach in form those of the negro. The same may be said of color. This indefiniteness of distinctions between different types is due to the variability of the types, which has been described before, and to the comparatively small differences between the types.

To give an instance. Negroes have thick lips. Nevertheless the thickness is not the same among all of them. In some cases it is quite small, in others very large. Europeans have thin lips, but we can find individuals whose lips have very considerable thickness. Thus it happens that there are some negroes whose lips deviate from the normal type in being unusually thin, and whose lips are therefore similar to those of Europeans whose lips are unusually thick. The less distinct two types are, the greater will be the number of individuals in both groups that are alike. It follows also, from what has been said, that the greater the variability of each type, the greater will be the probability that some individuals of the two types compared will be alike. We may perhaps best express this by saying that the varieties constituting each race overlap. In many cases, and in some of those that are most important for our inquiry, this overlapping is extended. Thus I have pointed out the differences in average brain-weight between different races. Brain-weights are, however, so variable, that a considerable overlapping occurs, and that even the average sizes of the brains of the white race are numerously represented among other races. Medium-sized brains of whites may be represented by the group of individuals having skull capacities of from 1450 cc. to 1650 cc. This group embraces 55 per cent of the Europeans, 58 per cent of the African negroes, and 58 per cent of the Melanesians. The same result appears when we compare the number of individuals having great cranial capacities. We find that 50 per cent of all whites have a capacity of the skull greater than 1550 cc., while 27 per cent of the negroes and 32 per cent of the Melanesians have capacities above this value. If we were to assume a direct relation between size of brain and ability, — which, as we have seen before, is not admissible, — we might, at most, anticipate a lack of men of high genius, but should not expect any great lack of faculty among the great mass of negroes living among the whites, and enjoying the advantages of the leadership of the best men of that race.

On the other hand, we find characteristics in different races so far apart and so little variable, that an overlapping is entirely or practically excluded. Examples of these are the frizzly hair of the negro as compared with the straight hair of the Mongol; the elevation and narrowness of the nose of the Armenian, and the flatness of the negro nose; the differences in pigmentation of the North European and of the Central African.

Investigations on the character of variability, which

have been based on the measurements of the body, on social and economic phenomena, and also on variable physical phenomena, such as meteorological data, have resulted in the discovery that almost always the same law nearly covers the distribution of the numerical values of the observations (Lock, Bowley).

It has been shown that the values which represent the phenomenon are so distributed that certain numerical values occur very frequently, and that the greater the difference between an observation and the value at which the greatest number of cases are found, the less will be the number of these observations. The character of this

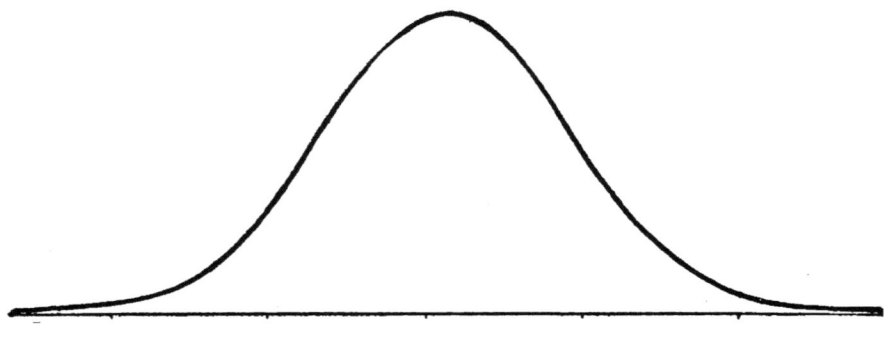

FIG. 1.

distribution is shown in Fig. 1, in which the horizontal line represents the numerical values of the observations, while the vertical distances represent the frequency of that observation to which the vertical distance belongs.

In the theoretical distribution which is represented in Fig. 1, the following values of the stature of a number of men are found : —

1415–1455 mm	5 cases
1455–1495 mm	11 cases
1495–1535 mm	44 cases
1535–1575 mm, ...	135 cases
1575–1615 mm, ...	325 cases
1615–1655 mm	607 cases
1655–1695 mm, ...	882 cases
1695–1735 mm, ...	1000 cases
1735–1775 mm	882 cases
1775–1815 mm, ...	607 cases
1815–1855 mm, ...	325 cases
1855–1895 mm, ...	135 cases
1895–1935 mm	44 cases
1935–1975 mm	11 cases
1975–2015 mm	5 cases

When we compare two series of this class which are grouped around different values, they may overlap each other. For instance, in a people of tall stature and another one of lower stature, the following theoretical distribution of numerical values of stature would be possible : —

I	II	
1415–1455 mm.	1425–1455 mm.	. . . . . . 5 cases
1455–1495 mm.	1455–1485 mm.	. . . . . . 11 cases
1495–1535 mm.	1485–1515 mm.	. . . . . . 44 cases
1535–1575 mm.	1515–1545 mm.	. . . . . 135 cases
1575–1615 mm.	1545–1575 mm.	. . . . . 325 cases

I	II		
1615–1655 mm.	1575–1605 mm.	. . . . .	607 cases
1655–1695 mm.	1605–1635 mm.	. . . . .	882 cases
1695–1735 mm.	1635–1665 mm.	. . . . .	1000 cases
1735–1775 mm.	1665–1695 mm.	. . . . .	882 cases
1775–1815 mm.	1695–1725 mm.	. . . . .	607 cases
1815–1855 mm.	1725–1755 mm.	. . . . .	325 cases
1855–1895 mm.	1755–1785 mm.	. . . . .	135 cases
1895–1935 mm.	1785–1815 mm.	. . . . . .	44 cases
1935–1975 mm.	1815–1845 mm.	. . . . . .	11 cases
1975–2015 mm.	1845–1875 mm.	. . . . . .	5 cases

In these two series the group of statures from 1575 mm.
to 1695 mm. occurs 1814 times in the first series, 3371
times in the second; that is to say, 1814 individuals are
found in both classes, and 1557 (i.e., 3371 − 1814) are found

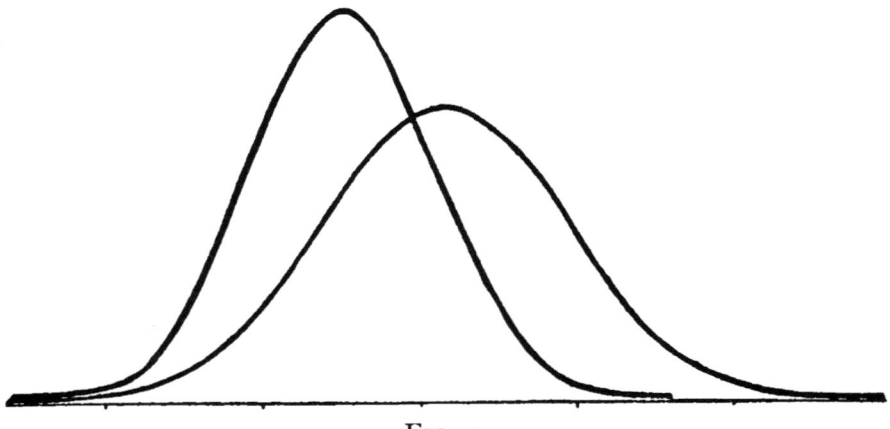

FIG. 2.

only in the class of people of tall stature. In Fig. 2
I have represented these two series in one system of co-
ordinates. Evidently all the individuals who belong to

both series, and who are shown in the surface enclosed between both curves, are found in both series; and only the others, who are outside of this surface, and who belong to one of the groups, are not found in the other one.

Bearing in mind these facts relating to types and variability, we are in a position to turn to a consideration of the characteristics of primitive man and of civilized man, and of members of distinct races.

We will first direct our attention to the differences between civilized man and primitive man, both being members of the same race. For the white race this difference can no longer be observed, because there are no primitive white men in the strict sense of the term. Nevertheless we may discover certain analogues. Some of the peasants in the remote mountain districts of southeastern Europe do not live in a manner so very different from the way of living of what we ordinarily call primitive people; for the mode of life of the agricultural Indians of North America at the time of Columbus, or that of some agricultural negro tribes, is, so far as nutrition and occupation are concerned, quite similar to theirs. Also some of the fishermen on the coast of Europe may well be compared, in their mode of life, with the fishermen of America or Asia. More direct comparisons may be made among the people of eastern Asia, where we may contrast the cultured Chinese and the primitive Amur River tribes, the northern Japanese and the Ainu, the civilized Malay and the mountain tribes of Sumatra or the Philippines. Similar comparisons are possible for the negro race when we contrast the small educated class of negroes in America and the African tribesmen; and for the American race when we compare the educated Indians, particularly of Spanish America, and the tribes of the prairies and of the virgin forests.

It is obvious that in all these cases we are comparing groups of the same descent, but living in distinct economic, social, and other environmental conditions. If we find differences among them, they can only be due, directly or indirectly, to environment. Thus the fundamental problem presents itself, In how far are human types stable, in how far variable under the influences of environment?

It is difficult to take up this inquiry on the basis of a direct comparison between primitive and civilized types belonging to the same races, partly because material is hard to obtain, partly because the homogeneity of the race is often open to doubt; but it is at once apparent that every inquiry into the variability of human types living under the effect of different types of environment will help us to gain an insight into the question at issue, so that we are led to a more general discussion of the problem of the stability or variability of the form of the human body.

The principles of biological science forbid us to assume a permanent stability of bodily form. Our whole modern concept of the development of varieties and of species is based on the assumption of cumulative or sudden variation. The variations that have been found in the human body are quite in accordance with this view, and I may quote here a few words from Wiedersheim's admirable treatise on the structure of man as an index of his past history: "In the course of Phylogeny the body of Man has undergone a series of modifications which still in part find expression in his ontogeny. There are indications that changes in his organization are still continuing, and that the Man of the future will be different from the Man of to-day." The best illustrations of those changes are found in the forms of organs which are undergoing reduction. Thus we may observe that in modern man the little toe is often two-jointed, a phenomenon presumably due to lack of functional use. This condition has been observed in races going barefooted as well as in those wearing shoes, so that it cannot be ascribed to artificial causes. The teeth also show a tendency to gradual reduction, especially in the variable size of the molars and of the upper outer incisors. The third molar, or wisdom tooth, is often retained, and is in most races considerably reduced in size. Retention or slight development of the upper outer incisor is also of frequent occurrence. A similar reduction may be observed at the lower end of the thorax, where the development of ribs and sternum shows great variations.

The significance of these phenomena lies in the fact that in the evolutionary series the abnormal occurrences, which are found in different races in varying frequency, appear as new developments, which, if they should become normal, would increase the differentiation between man and the lower forms. The actual proof of increasing frequency of these features, and of their becoming permanent characteristics, has not been given, but seems more than plausible.

This inference is strongly supported by the occurrence of rudimentary, functionless organs, and by the temporary appearance of lower features during ontogenetic development.

It has been shown that some of these reductions — like the retention of outer incisors — are hereditary, and thus liable to perpetuate themselves. To a certain extent this explains the observation that certain variations occur with greater frequency among primitive tribes than in civilized man. Most primitive tribes are very small in numbers, or for long periods, during which they increased in numbers, have had little intercourse with foreign people. If in such a group any of the original families showed a certain peculiarity, it must now be found more frequently than in any other tribes. A case of this kind is the frequency of supernumerary vertebræ among the Indians of Vancouver Island, and probably also the frequency of the *torus palatinus* among the Lapps. It may be left an open question, whether the frequent occurrence of the *os Incæ* among the Pueblo Indians and Peruvians may be explained by the same consideration. Therefore it may be that the greater variability of certain races, in regard to these phenomena, is not an expression of a lower or higher degree of development of the whole group, as the case may be, but of the presence of a great number of members of a family which possessed the peculiar character. We do not deal in these cases with spontaneous variations, but with their hereditary re-appearance. In other words, if we are to admit the conclusion that greater variability means a lower or higher stage of development, it will be necessary first to prove that these variations appear spontaneously in any member of the group, and do not belong to certain families in which the feature is hereditary. Otherwise it will be necessary to prove that in larger groups of mankind the families exhibiting the particular anomaly had a greater probability of surviving than others.

However this may be, the occurrence of these variations shows that man cannot be assumed to have a stable form. It is of course an entirely open question, how long a time may be required to fix any one of the variations that we are here discussing.

The general tendency of anthropological inquiry has been to assume the permanence of the anatomical characteristics of the present races, beginning with the European races of the early neolithic times. Kollmann, the most pronounced advocate of this theory, claims that the oldest remains of man found in the neolithic deposits of Europe represent types which are still found unchanged among the modern civilized population of the continent. He has tried to identify all the varieties found in the neolithic prehistoric population with those living at the present time.

All studies of the distribution of head-forms and of other

anthropometric traits have shown uniformity over considerable continuous areas and through long periods; and the natural inference has been that heredity controls anthropometric forms, and that these are therefore stable (Deniker).

There is only one exception to this rule. In all cases in which the anthropometric traits undergo very considerable changes during the period of growth, the influence of favorable or unfavorable causes makes itself felt. The investigations conducted by Gould and Baxter during the war of the Rebellion have shown that the representatives of European nationalities born in America have statures higher than the representatives of the same nationalities born in Europe; and it has been assumed that better nutrition, or perhaps better hygienic and economic conditions in general, might increase the stature of a people. These conclusions were confirmed by Bowditch's measurements of the school-children of Boston, and by Peckham's anthropometric work in Milwaukee. These changes in stature, due to changed conditions, have recently been demonstrated also in Europe, where Ammon has shown that the population of Baden has materially increased in size during the last thirty years. Other corroborative evidence has been obtained from the study of various social classes, in which Bowditch found an increase of stature, beginning with the children of unskilled laborers, and increasing among those of skilled laborers, members of the mercantile class and of the professional class; and from the observations showing a correlation between the character of streets occupied by the well-to-do and the poor, and the stature of their inhabitants (Ripley). Nevertheless these changes of stature were not interpreted as changes in type, because they may well be understood to be due to the elimination of retarding influences, which prevent many individuals from attaining their normal growth.

The results of the observations on stature are substantiated by other anthropometrical studies of various occupations. The best-authenticated fact, because based on the greatest number of observations, is the difference in type between sailors and soldiers who were measured during the war of the Rebellion. It was found that sailors had legs as long as those of the negroes, and correspondingly a shorter trunk, while their arms were equally as long as those of the soldiers of the army. We may also call to mind the investigations carried on in the gymnasiums of our colleges, which show that a series of measurements which depend largely upon the functions of groups of muscles change very rapidly under the influence of practice. It will be acknowledged at once that differences in the use of muscles during childhood, and continued in later life, must result in differences of structure, either permanent, or at least temporary.

A study of the conditions of growth shows how such changes in the form of the body must develop. Setting aside the prenatal development, we find that at the time of birth some parts of the body are so fully developed that they are not far removed from their final size, while others are quite undeveloped. Thus the skull is, comparatively speaking, large at the time of birth, grows rapidly for a short time, but very soon approaches its full size, and then continues to grow very slowly. The limbs, on the other hand, grow rapidly for many years. Other organs do not begin their rapid development until much later in life. Thus it happens that retarding or accelerating influences acting upon the body at different periods of growth may have quite different results. After the head has nearly completed its growth, retarding influences may still influence the length of the limbs. The face, which grows rapidly for a longer period than the cranium, can be influenced later than the latter. In short, the influence of environment may be the more marked, the less developed

the organ that is subject to it.   Data on the unequal
rate of growth of different parts of the body have been
furnished by Weissenberg.

The influence of retardation, so far as it has been
studied, seems to be lasting.   In other words, a retardation in development is never completely made good by
long-continued development.   When a child, through unfavorable influences, has grown slowly during a number
of years, it will probably continue to grow longer than
other, normal children ; but the total amount of its growth
will always remain too small (Boas and Wissler).   On
the other hand, children whose development has been ac-
celerated will reach the adult stage early, but nevertheless
the total amount of their growth will be relatively great.
It follows from this consideration of the effect of retardation and of difference in period, that not only the absolute
size, but also the relative proportions, of the body, must
be influenced by periods of retardation or acceleration.

The whole trend of the studies of growth thus emphasizes the importance of the effect of rate of development
upon the final form of the body.   Illness in early childhood, malnutrition, lack of fresh air and physical exer-
cise, are so many retarding causes, which bring it about
that the growing individual of a certain age is in its

physiological development younger than the healthy, well-nourished individual, who has plenty of fresh air, and who puts his muscular system to good use. Retardation or acceleration has, however, the effect of modifying the later course of development ; so that the final stage will be the more favorable, the less the retarding causes.

It seems more than likely, judging from the course of development of a few simple mental activities that have been made the subject of study, that mental development follows laws quite analogous to those of physical development (Meumann).

These facts relating to growth are of fundamental importance for a correct interpretation of the oft-discussed phenomena of early arrest of growth. We have seen that among members of the same race a prolonged period of growth goes hand in hand with unfavorable development, while an abbreviated period of growth results in larger dimensions of all physical measurements, and in a superiority of mental activity. In this statement pathological cases of complete premature arrest of development, or of over-development, are of course excluded, — cases of dwarfish growth or of microcephaly, as well as cases of hypertrophic growth of organs. It follows, that, in judging the physiological value of arrest of growth, the mere fact that growth ceases in one race at an earlier time than in another cannot be considered as significant in itself without observations on the rapidity of growth.

So far, the question still remains open, in how far there may be changes in the types of man that cannot be explained by acceleration or retardation of growth.

An attempt has been made by Rieger to explain differences in head-form as due to the effect of physiological and mechanical conditions, and Engel emphasizes the effect of pressure of the muscles upon the forms of the head. Walcher tries to explain different head-forms by the consideration of the position of the infant in the cradle. He believes that position on the back produces round heads; position on the side, long heads. It would seem, however, that the difference of head-form in large areas of Europe, in which infants are treated in the same manner, are too great to make this explanation acceptable.

A number of observations have been made, however, which demonstrate conclusively a difference between urban and rural types. These observations were first made by Ammon, who showed that the urban population in Baden differs from the rural population in head-form, stature, and pigmentation. He accepts the conclusion that we have here an actual change in type ; due, however, not to a direct effect of environment, but rather to an elimination of certain types in city life : in other words, an effect of natural selection. This observation is in accord with observations made by Livi in the cities of Italy, which show also a difference when compared to the surrounding country. Comparisons of the normal and hospital populations of London, made by Shrubsall, are not unfavorable to the assumption of a certain amount of correlation between morbidity and physical type, although the homogeneity of material from a metropolis like London, drawn from different social strata of a large city, remains always open to doubt.

Another explanation, given by Livi, seems to account adequately for the difference between city and country population, without necessitating the assumption of any considerable effect of natural selection, which presupposes an improbable correlation between mortality and fertility on the one hand, and traits like head-form and pigmentation on the other. The change of type in cities, so far as it has been observed, is of such character, that the city always shows greater resemblance to the average type of the whole large district in which it is located. If the local rural population is markedly short-headed, the general type over a larger area from which the city population is drawn more long-headed, then the city population will be more long-headed, and *vice versa*. Unless selection can be demonstrated to occur in a sufficient number of definite families, this explanation seems simpler and adequate.

Up to quite recent times no evidence of actual changes of type was available, except the observations by Ammon and those by Livi on the physical characteristics of rural and urban populations, to which I have just referred, and some others on the influence of altitude upon physical form. In the discussions of the distribution of different types of man in Europe, peculiarities of body-form in certain areas — as in the mountains of central France, in parts of Tuscany, in the province of Zealand in Holland, in southwestern Norway — have been explained as due to the survival of old racial types, to the influence of natural selection, or to the direct influence of environment, according as the necessities of the case prompted the investigator to adduce the one cause or the other, or a combination of any two or of all, as a convenient explanation of the difficult phenomenon (Ripley). It goes without saying that haphazard application of unproved though possible theories cannot serve as proof of the effectiveness of selection or of environment in modifying types. The effectiveness of selection can be proved only by an investigation of the surviving members of a type as compared to those eliminated by death, or of a shifting of population connected with the selection of a certain type. The influence of environment requires the direct comparison of parents living under one environment with children living under another environment.

I cannot give any example in which the influence of selection has been proved beyond cavil. It seems plausible that in the criminal colonies of earlier periods, and in the settling of the West by the most vigorous members of our Eastern population, and in the complementary weeding-out of strong elements in some parts of New England, this principle may have been active ; but we have no actual data which would connect with physical types the selection that has undoubtedly taken place.

On the other hand, it has been my good fortune to be able to demonstrate the existence of a direct influence of environment upon the bodily form of man by a comparison of immigrants born in Europe and their descendants born in New York City (Boas). I have investigated four groups of people, — the South Italians, representing the Mediterranean type of Europe, which is characterized by short stature, elongated head, dark complexion and hair; the Central European type, which is characterized by medium stature, short head, light hair and lighter complexion; the Northwest European type, which is characterized by tall stature, elongated head, light complexion, and blond hair. Furthermore, I have investigated an extended series of East European Hebrews, who resemble in some respects the Central European group. The traits which I selected for examination are head-measurements, stature, weight, and hair-color. Among these, only stature and weight are closely related to the rate of growth, while head-measurements and hair-color are only slightly subjected to these influences. Differences in hair-color and head-development do not belong to the group of measurements of which I spoke before, which depend in their final values upon the physiological conditions during the period of growth. From all we know, they are primarily dependent upon heredity.

The results of our inquiry have led to the unexpected result that the American-born descendants of these types differ from their parents; and that these differences develop in early childhood, and persist throughout life. It is furthermore remarkable that each type changes in a peculiar way. The head of the American-born Sicilian becomes rounder than that of the foreign-born. This is due to a loss in length and an increase in width. The face becomes narrower, the stature and weight decrease. The head of the American-born Central European loses both in length and width, more so in width, and thus becomes more elongated. The face decreases very much in width; stature and weight increase. The modifications of the American-born descendants of the Scotch type are not marked, except that stature and weight increase. The American-born Hebrew has a longer and narrower head than the European-born; the head is therefore considerably more elongated. His face is narrower; stature and weight are increased. In none of the types have marked differences in color of hair between American-born and foreign-born been found.

In order to understand the causes which bring about these alterations of type, it is necessary to know how long a time must have elapsed since the immigration of the parents before a noticeable change of type of the offspring is brought about. This investigation has been carried out mainly for the cephalic index, which, during the period of growth of the individual, undergoes only slight modifications. The investigation of the Hebrews shows very clearly that the cephalic index of the foreign-born is practically the same, no matter how old the individual at the time of immigration.   This might be expected when the immigrants are adult or nearly mature ; but it is of interest to note that even children who come here when one year or a few years old develop the cephalic index characteristic of the foreign-born.   This index ranges around 83. When we compare the value of this index with that of the index of the American-born, according to the time elapsed since their immigration, we find a sudden change.   The value drops to about 82 for those born immediately after the immigration of their parents, and drops to 79 in the second generation ; i.e., among the children of American-born children of immigrants.   In other words, the effect of American environment makes itself felt immediately, and increases slowly with the increase of time elapsed between the immigration of the parents and the birth of the child.

The conditions among the Sicilians and Neapolitans are quite similar to those observed among the Hebrews. The cephalic index of the foreign-born remains throughout on almost the same level.   Those born in America immediately after the arrival of their parents show an increase of the cephalic index.   In this case, the transition, although rapid, is not quite so sudden as among the Hebrews, probably because among those born a year before or after immigration there is some doubt as to the place of their birth. These uncertainties are due to the habit of the Italians to migrate back and forth between Italy and America before finally settling here, and to the indefiniteness of their answers in regard to the places of birth of the child, which sometimes had to be inferred from the age of the child and the year of immigration of the mother. As long as this uncertainty exists, which is hardly present at all in the data relating to the Hebrews, it does not seem necessary to assume any other cause for the more gradual change of the cephalic index about the time of immigration.

The Italian immigration is so recent, that individuals who were born many years after the arrival of their parents in America are very few in number, and no individuals of the second generation have been observed. For this reason it is hardly possible to decide whether the increase of the cephalic index continues with the length of time elapsed between the immigration of the parents and the birth of the child.

The explanation of these remarkable phenomena is not easy. Whatever their causes may be, the change in form cannot be doubted. It might, however, be claimed that the changes are not due to deep physiological causes, but to the changes of certain external factors. The composition of the immigrant population might be such that the people who came here at different periods had distinct physical characteristics, and that these are now reflected in the descendants of the older generations when compared with the more recent immigrants. It can be shown, however, that the differences between the Hebrews who immigrated at different periods between 1860 and 1909 are so slight that they cannot account for the type of the descendants of immigrants. This important point can be elucidated more definitely by the application of a different method. For this purpose I have compared the cephalic index of all immigrants of a certain year with that of their descendants. It appears from these comparisons that the differences which are exhibited by the whole series exist also between the immigrants who arrived here in a certain year and their descendants. This purely statistical explanation of the phenomenon may therefore be dismissed.

More difficult to investigate is the hypothesis that the mechanical treatment of infants may have a decided influence upon the form of the head, and that the changes in cradling and bedding which are made by some immigrants almost immediately after their arrival in America account for the changes of head-form. If this were true, the continued changes among the Hebrews might indicate merely that the American method of cradling is used the more frequently, the longer the family has resided in this country. A number of investigators have claimed that the position of the child on the back tends to produce short-headedness, and that the position on the side tends to produce long-headedness (Walcher). There is good evidence that a flattening of the occiput occurs when a very hard pillow is used and the child lies permanently on its back. This is the case, for instance, among many Indian tribes, and similar results might obtain if a swathed child were to lie permanently on its back. The prevalence of rachitis in New York would favor distortion due to pressure.

While I cannot disprove the existence of such influences, I think weighty considerations are against their acceptance. If we assume that among the Hebrews the children born abroad have a lesser length of head than those born here because they are swathed and lie more permanently on their backs than the American-born children, who can move about freely, we must conclude that there is a certain compensatory decrease in the other diameters of the head of the American-born. Since this compensation is distributed in all directions, its amount in any one direction will be very small (Boas).

The decrease in the width of head that has been observed is so large that it cannot be considered simply as an effect of compensation; but we have to make the additional hypothesis that the American-born children lie so much on their sides that a narrowing of the head is brought about by mechanical pressure. The same considerations hold good in all the other types. If, therefore, in one case the greater freedom of position of the child increases the length of its head, it is difficult to see why, among the Bohemians, the same causes should decrease both horizontal diameters of the head, and why, among the Sicilians, the length should decrease, the width increase.

The development of the width of the face seems to my mind to show most clearly that it is not the mechanical treatment of the infant that brings about the changes in question. The cephalic index suffers a very slight decrease from the second year to adult life. It is therefore evident that children who arrive in America very young cannot be much affected by American environment in regard to their cephalic index. On the other hand, if we consider a measurement that increases appreciably during the period of growth, we may expect that in children born abroad but removed to America when young, the total growth may be modified by American environment. The best material for this study is presented by the Bohemians, among whom there are relatively many full-grown American-born individuals. The width of face of Bohemians, when arranged according to their ages at the time of immigration, shows that there is a loss among those who came here as young children, — the greater, the younger they were. Continuing this comparison with the Americans born one, two, and more years after the arrival of their mothers, the width of face is seen to decrease still further. It appears, therefore, that the American environment causes a retardation of the growth of the width of face at a period when mechanical influences are no longer possible.

I have not carried through the analogous investigation for stature, because in this case the increase might simply be ascribed to the better nutrition of most of the north and central European immigrants after their immigration into this country.

There is another hypothesis which might account for the observed changes of type. If it were assumed that among the descendants of immigrants born in America there are an appreciable number who are in reality children of American fathers, not of their reputed fathers, a general assimilation by the American type would occur. Socially this condition is not at all plausible; but, on account of the importance of the phenomenon that we are discussing, it should be considered. I do not think that any of the observations that have been made are in favor of this theory. The changes that occur in the Bohemians who arrive here as young children, the different directions of the changes in distinct types, particularly the shortening of the head of Bohemians and of Italians, do not favor the assumption. Furthermore, if the modifications were due to race-mixture, the similarity between fathers and American-born children should be less than the similarity between fathers and foreign-born children, but there is no indication that this is the case.

This hypothesis is also shown to be untenable by the comparisons of fathers and mothers with their own foreign-born children. These comparisons show that the differences are the same in the case of fathers and children, and of mothers and children; so that obviously the same conditions must control the relations between fathers and their children, and mothers and their children. In other words, the fathers must be considered as the true fathers of their children.

Earnest advocates of the theory of selection might claim that all these changes are due to the effects of changes in death-rate among foreign-born and American-born; that either abroad or here individuals of certain types are more liable to die, and that thus these changes are gradually brought about. On the whole, it seems to my mind, the burden of proof would lie entirely on those who claim such a correlation between head-index, width of face, etc., and death-rate, — a correlation which I think is highly improbable, and which could be proposed only to sustain the theory of selection, not on account of any available facts. I grant the desirability of settling the question by actual observations; but, until these are available, we may point out that the very suddenness of the changes after immigration, and the absence of changes due to selection by mortality among the adult foreign-born, would require such a complicated adjustment of cause and effect in regard to the correlation of mortality and bodily form, that the theory would become improbable on account of its complexity.

It would be saying too much to claim that all the distinct European types become the same in America, without mixture, solely by the action of the new environment. First of all, I have investigated only the effect of one environment, and there is every reason to believe that a number of distinct types are developing in America ; but we will set aside this point, and discuss only our New York observations. Although the long-headed Sicilian becomes more round-headed in New York, the round-headed Bohemian and Hebrew more long-headed, the approach to a uniform general type cannot be established, because we do not know yet how long the changes continue, and whether they would all lead to the same result. I confess, I do not consider such a result as likely, because the proof of the plasticity of types does not imply that the plasticity is unlimited. The history of the British types in America, of the Dutch in the East Indies, of the Spaniards in South America, favors the assumption of a strictly limited plasticity. Certainly our discussion should be based on this more conservative basis until an unexpectedly wide range of variability of types can be proved. It is one of the most important problems that arise out of this investigation, to determine how far the instability or plasticity of types may extend.

Whatever the extent of these bodily changes may be, if we grant the correctness of our inferences in regard to the plasticity of human types, we are necessarily led to grant also a great plasticity of the mental make-up of human types. We have observed that features of the body which have almost obtained their final form at the time of birth show modifications of great importance in new surroundings. We have seen that others which increase during the whole period of growth, and are therefore subject to the continued effect of the new environment, are modified even among individuals who arrived here during their childhood. From these facts we must conclude that the fundamental traits of the mind, which are closely correlated with the physical condition of the body, and whose development continues over many years after physical growth has ceased, are the more subject to far-reaching changes. It is true that this is a conclusion by inference; but if we have succeeded in proving changes in the form of the body, the burden of proof will rest on those who, notwithstanding those changes, continue to claim the absolute permanence of other forms and functions of the body.

In order to gain a correct understanding of the importance of changes in the frame of the human body, it seems desirable to view the type of modern man from a somewhat different standpoint.

It is quite a number of years since Fritsch, in his studies of the anthropology of South Africa, pointed out that a peculiar difference exists in the form of the body of the Bushman and the Hottentot as compared to that of Europeans, in that the former exhibit slenderer forms of the bones, that the bone is very solid in its structure; while in the European the skeleton appears heavier, but of more open structure. Similar differences may be observed in a comparison between the skeletons of wild animals and those of domesticated animals; and this observation has led to the conclusion that the Bushmen are in their physical habitus to a certain extent like wild animals, while the Europeans resemble in their structure domesticated animals.

This point of view — namely, that the human race in its civilized forms must be compared, not with the forms of wild animals, but rather with those of domesticated animals — seems to me a very important one; and a somewhat detailed study of the conditions in which various races are found suggests that at the present time, even among the most primitive types of man, changes incident to domestication have taken place almost all over the world.

There are three different types of changes due to domestication which must be clearly distinguished. On the one hand, the bodies of domesticated animals undergo

considerable transformations, owing to the change in nutrition and use of the body. On the other hand, selection
and crossing have played an important part in the development of races of domesticated animals.

Some changes of the former class are due to the more
regular and more ample nutrition; other changes are
due to modifications of the kinds of food which the
domesticated animal uses when compared with the
wild animal of the same species; still others are due
to the different manner in which the muscular and the
nervous systems are put into use. These changes are not
quite the same among carnivorous and among herbivorous animals. The dog and the cat, for instance, are fairly
regularly fed when they are found in domestication; but
the food which is given to them is of a quite different
character from the food which the wild dog and cat eat.
Even among people whose diet consists almost entirely
of meat, dogs are generally fed with boiled meat, or rather
with the boiled, less nutritious parts of animals; while,
among other tribes which utilize to a great extent vegetable food, dogs are often fed with mush and other vegetable material. The same is true of our cats, whose
diet is not by any means entirely a meat diet. The
exertions which wild carnivorous animals undergo to

obtain food are incomparably greater than those of domesticated carnivorous animals; and it is obvious that for this reason the muscular system and the central nervous system may undergo considerable changes.

The muscular exertions of herbivorous animals, so far as they are fed on pastures, are not so materially changed. The grazing habits of cattle and sheep in domestication are about the same as the grazing habits of wild animals of the same class; but the rapid movements and the watchfulness required for protecting the herd against carnivorous animals have completely disappeared. Stable-fed animals live under highly artificial conditions, and material changes may occur in them.

I think the changes due to these causes may be observed in the oldest types of domesticated animals, such as are found in the neolithic villages of Europe, in which native European species appear in domesticated form (Keller). They may also be observed in the dogs of the various continents, which differ markedly from the wild species from which they are derived. Even the Eskimo dog, which is a descendant of the gray wolf and still interbreeds with the gray wolf, differs in bodily form from the wild animal (Beckmann). Modifications may also be observed in newly domesticated animals, like the Chukchee reindeer, which differs in type from the wild reindeer of the same area (Bogoras). I think it very unlikely, judging from our knowledge of the methods of domestication of tribes like the Eskimo and Chukchee, that any material amount of selection has contributed to the modifications of form which are found in these races of primitive domesticated animals. Their uniformity is still fairly well marked, although they have assumed types different from the wild species.

A more marked differentiation of domesticated forms does not seem to occur until man begins to select and to isolate, more or less consciously, particular breeds. Opportunity for such isolation has been the greater, the older the domestication of any particular species. We find, therefore, that the number of distinct breeds have come to be greatest in those animals which have been under domestication for the longest periods.

The number of varieties of domesticated species has also been increased by unintentional or intentional crossing of different species, from which are derived many breeds whose ancestry it is often so difficult to unravel.

It appears, therefore, that there are three distinct causes which bring about the development of different types in domesticated animals : first, the influence of change of nutrition and mode of life; secondly, conscious selection; and, thirdly, crossing.

Among these causes, the first and the third have been most strongly active in the development of the races of man. The condition of the tribes of man the world over is such, that there are only very few whose mode of nutrition is analogous to that of wild animals, and a consideration of the stages of human culture shows that similar conditions have prevailed for a long period. I think we may safely say that in all those cases in which man practises agriculture, when he is the owner of herds of domesticated animals which are used for food, the food-supply has become regular, and is obtained by an application of the muscular system in highly specialized directions. Examples of this condition are, for instance, the central African negroes, who have their gardens near their villages, the cultivation of the gardens being essentially the work of the women, while the men are engaged in various specialized industrial pursuits. Neither is the manner of the use of the body which is applied by wild animals for protection against enemies found among these tribes. The manner of combat is one in which muscular strength alone is not decisive, but where excellence of weapons and strategy count as much as mere strength and agility.

The conditions among the American agricultural Indians of the Mississippi Valley or of those of the South American forests are similar in character.

As an example of a pastoral people among whom considerable regularity in nutrition obtains, we might mention the reindeer-breeders of Siberia or the cattle-breeders of Africa.

We know, of course, that among all these people, periods of starvation occur, due to a failure of the crops or to epidemics in the herds; but the normal condition is one of fairly regular and ample food-supply.

The conditions among fishing tribes are not very different; and we find that, owing to methods of storing provisions, and to the superabundance of food-supply obtained in one season and sufficient to last for the rest of the year, the nutrition of these people is also fairly regular. In this case, also, the kind of muscular exertion required for obtaining food is specialized, and differs from that required from the simple pursuit of game.

The only modern tribes among which the effects of civilization on bodily activities are slight are those who, like the Bushmen of South Africa, the Australians, the Eskimo of Arctic America, the Veddahs of Ceylon, obtain their livelihood by the constant, daily-repeated pursuit of animals, or by the gathering of plants or small invertebrates which grow scattered over a wide area.

Connected with these conditions are also the characteristic selections of food-stuffs by different tribes, such as the exclusive meat diet of some tribes (perhaps most pronounced among the Eskimo) and the exclusive vegetable diet of others, well developed, for instance, in southern Asia. Both of these have, in all probability, a far-reaching effect upon the bodily form of these races.

The second group of causes which is most potent in developing distinct races of domesticated animals –- namely, conscious selection — has probably never been very active in the races of man. We do not know of a single case in which it can be shown that intermarriage between distinct types of the same descent was prohibited ; and whatever selection there may have been in the development of primitive society seems to have been rather that type of natural selection which encourages the mating of like with like, or such intricate selection as is due to the social laws of intermarriage, which prevented intermarriages of relatives of certain grades, and often also of members of different generations. Thus a very common form of marriage restriction brings it about that among certain tribes the children of brother and sister intermarry, while the children of brothers and the children of sisters are not allowed to intermarry. Similar restrictions are found in great number, and may possibly have had a certain selective effect, although their operation can hardly be assumed to have had very marked results upon the form of the human body (Pearson).

In some cases social laws have had the indirect effect of perpetuating distinctions between separate parts of a population, or at least of retarding their complete amalgamation. This is the case where laws of endogamy relate to groups of distinct descent, and may be observed, for instance, among the castes of Bengal, where the low castes are of the characteristic South Indian type, while the highest castes preserve the type of the tribes of northwestern India (Risley and Gait). The numerous intermediate castes show, however, that the laws of endogamy, even where they are as stringent as those of India, cannot prevent blood-mixture. Whether or not in extreme cases endogamy in small groups, as among the ancient Egyptians, has led to the development of well-defined types, is a question that cannot be answered; but it is certain that none of these types, when found in a large population, have survived.

The third element of domestication, on the other hand,

has probably been very important in the development of the races of man. Crossings between distinct types are so markedly common in the history of primitive people, and so markedly rare in the history of wild animals, that in this case the analogy between domesticated animals and man becomes very clear. Cases of hybrid forms in nature are almost everywhere rare; while, as I have pointed out before, domesticated animals have been crossed and recrossed without end. Crossings between the most distinct types of man are also of very common occurrence. As an instance, I might mention the inter-marriages between the Hamitic tribes of the Sahara and the negro tribes of the Soudan (Nachtigal); the mixtures between the Negritos and Malay, which are of such common occurrence in the Malay Peninsula (Martin), and which are probably to a great extent the cause of the peculiar distribution of types in the whole Malay Archi-pelago; the mixtures which have taken place in Fiji; that of the Ainu and Japanese in the northern part of Japan; of European and Mongol in eastern Europe; not to speak of the more recent mixtures between European and other races which were incident to the gradual distribution of the European race over the whole world.

This point of view — namely, the consideration of man

as a domesticated being (with the sole exception, perhaps, of a few hunting tribes) — is also of great importance for a clear understanding of his mental activities. The behavior of primitive domesticated animals, like that of the Eskimo dog or of the Chukchee reindeer, is decidedly different from the behavior of wild animals. We might perhaps say that the range of mentality of the domesticated forms seems to be, on the whole, wider, and this condition increases with increasing degree of domestication. Cases in which the mental activities of domesticated animals are more deficient than those of the wild animals, do occur, but are not as frequent as the reverse cases. An example of this kind is furnished by sheep.

We are thus led to the conclusion that environment has an important effect upon the anatomical structure and physiological functions of man; and that for this reason differences of type and action between primitive and civilized groups of the same race must be expected. It seems plausible that one of the most potent causes of these modifications must be looked for in the progressive domestication of man incident to the advance of civilization.

III. INFLUENCE OF HEREDITY UPON HUMAN TYPES

WE will now turn to the consideration of another element which determines the physical type of man. Although we have seen that environment, particularly domestication, has a far-reaching influence upon the bodily form of the races of man, these influences are of a quite secondary character when compared to the far-reaching influence of heredity. Even granting the greatest possible amount of influence to environment, it is readily seen that all the essential traits of man are due primarily to heredity. The descendants of the negro will always be negroes; the descendants of the whites, whites; and we may go even considerably further, and may recognize that the essential detailed characteristics of a type will always be reproduced in the descendants, although they may be modified to a considerable extent by the influence of environment. I am inclined to believe that the influence of environment is of such a character, that, although the same race may assume a different type when removed from one environment to another, it will revert to its old type when replaced in its old environment. This point has not been proved by actual anthropological evidence; but it seems reasonable to make this assumption by analogy with what we know of the behavior of plants and animals. It would, of course, be highly desirable to clear up this question by appropriate investigations.

In order to obtain a clearer understanding of the racial problem, it seems necessary to describe more definitely the characteristics of heredity. In the discussion of modern anthropology, two theories have been advocated relating to the manner in which parental traits are inherited by children. Francis Galton and his adherents have assumed that the form of the body of an individual is determined by the racial type to which the parents belong, modified, however, by the tendency of reversion to a type intermediate between the special variations presented by the parents. When, for instance, the father of an individual is unusually tall, his mother somewhat taller than the average, it is assumed that the tendency of the children would be to develop a stature which is somewhat near the general type, but at the same time dependent upon the intermediate value located between the stature of the mother and that of the father. On the other hand, the development of the Mendelian doctrine (Lock, Bateson) of heredity has led other investigators to assume that the offspring of two distinct types may be a mixed type, but that his descendants will tend to revert either to one parental type or to the other, or that one of the parental types may dominate over the influence of the other parental type.   Investigations relating to this problem are not very numerous; but, on the whole, it would appear that the results so far obtained are in favor rather of a modified form of Mendelian inheritance than of an inheritance characterized by reversion of the children to a middle type between the parents, or to a type dependent upon such a middle type.

A number of years ago I had an opportunity to investigate a considerable number of Indian half-bloods; that is to say, of descendants of Indian mothers and white fathers.   The most characteristic difference between the American Indian race and the European race, so far as these differences can be expressed in metrical form, is found in the width of the face.   An extensive series of measurements of width of face made among half-bloods showed conclusively that the width of face does not tend to range around a certain intermediate value located between the width of face of the white race and that of the

Indian race, but there was a decided tendency in the children to resemble either the Indian race or the white race; in other words, that feature of Mendelian inheritance which brings about the occurrence of mixed characteristics in the first hybrid generation was not found, but instead of this a decided tendency of reversion to either type, and to comparative rarity of intermediate forms. The results seem also to indicate that the Indian form in this mixture seems to dominate over the white form, but not in the Mendelian sense, which would require the presence of dominant features in a certain definite number of individuals, but only in the sense that the Indian type was a little more frequent than the European type, with the effect that the average width of face of the whole series was a little nearer to the Indian group than to the white group.

While this single observation is not by any means sufficient to determine fully the characteristic traits of heredity which govern the phenomenon in question, they indicate decidedly and beyond cavil that, in this case at least, we find what has been called by Karl Pearson "alternating inheritance." It is worth remarking that not all the features of the body of the half-blood Indian exhibit the same tendency; that, for instance, in the case of stature, a general increase in the stature of the mixed people over that of the pure races may be observed.

Attention has been called by Felix von Luschan to a similar phenomenon which occurs in the mixed population of southern Asia Minor, where he believes to have found an alternating inheritance of the head-form, particularly of the proportions between width and length of head; some of the people retaining the short, high head-forms of the Armenoid type of the interior of Asia Minor, while the others have the long, low head of the Semites of Syria.

For a clear understanding of the laws of heredity, it seems important to know whether a similar alternating inheritance occurs in marriages of members of the same type. I have been enabled to investigate this question by a study of the East European Hebrews living in New York. A simple consideration shows, that, if the children tend to follow a type intermediate between the type of their parents, then the children of one family will show the same degree of resemblance among themselves, no matter how great the difference between the parents; for, if they simply tend to reproduce a middle type, it would not make any difference whether the mother is excessively short and the father excessively tall, or whether both parents are of middle stature. In both of these cases the intermediate value would be the same, and we should therefore expect that the effect upon the children would be the same. If, on the other hand, there is any kind of alternation in inheritance, the effect upon the family would be quite different. We should expect, in a family of which both parents are near the typical average, to find the children also to be near this average. On the other hand, if the mother is excessively short and the father excessively tall, we should expect some of the children to follow the mother in regard to shortness of stature, others to follow the father in regard to tallness. It will therefore be seen that in the case of alternating inheritance, we must expect an increased variability among the children. The compilation of material obtained from several thousand families shows very definitely that the variability among children both of whose parents belong to the same racial type, even to the same local type, increases quite considerably with the increased difference of the parents; so that we may assume a decided tendency to alternating inheritance in these cases. There is, however, no evidence whatever of the dominance of one type over another.

Quite a number of investigations have been made in relation to the intensity of heredity of parents and of grandparents; and, notwithstanding the uncertainty of the quantitative result, it seems reasonably certain that the intensity of heredity for each parent may be expressed by the value of about one-third (Pearson, Boas). It is somewhat difficult to explain clearly the significance of this value. I may, however, briefly indicate it in the following manner. Provided the mother differs in her stature by an amount of 9 cm. from the racial norm, — for instance, if she is 9 cm. taller than the average individual, — then we may expect the child to be one-third of 9 cm., or 3 cm., above the average. It will thus be seen that if both parents differ in the same direction from the average, the effect of both will be cumulative; and if both differ from the average of their people by the same amount, the joint effect of the two parents may be expressed by the coefficient of about two-thirds. In case, for instance, both father and mother should be 9 cm. above the type average, we should expect the child to be about two-thirds of 9 cm., or 6 cm., above the average.

Although definite information on the amount of heredity of previous generations is not yet available, the probability seems to be that the grandparents have jointly an influence of about two-ninths, the great-grandparents jointly of about two twenty-sevenths, etc., upon the offspring.

When we study these problems according to statistical theories, and take into consideration the observations on the resemblance of brothers and sisters, it can be shown that the theory of alternating inheritance cannot be taken too literally; for, if there were an absolute reversion of any one trait to pure ancestral types, we might say that the probability would be very small that two brothers should happen to repeat the bodily form of the same ancestor, because the number of ancestors in remote generations is very large. In other words, there must be an additional cause of resemblance between brothers and sisters. It is possible to show, that in case the inheritance has the strength denoted before, and if bodily form of a certain generation were due only to alternating inheritance acting from parents, grandparents, great-grandparents, and so on, and directly upon the generation in question, and without an occurrence of the same individuals in various places in the line of ancestors, then the resemblance between brothers and sisters, or, as we say, between the members of a fraternity, would result in a degree of resemblance which is much lower than the one actually observed. When the total number of ancestors is small, the recurrence of the same forms would become more probable, and the similarity of the series would increase. On the whole, the data seem to be best explained if we assume that there is not only alternating inheritance, but also a direct dependence upon the combination of the two parental types.

I should like to repeat here that these results have not been obtained with absolute certainty, and that it seems improbable that the laws of heredity in regard to various ancestral traits are the same. I do not enter into a discussion of the question of in how far these traits follow the laws of Mendelian inheritance, — a question that cannot be answered definitely at the present time (Davenport).

These problems have a fundamental importance for a clearer interpretation of the conditions which prevail in the form of local types of man.

In a large population which is as little stable in its habits as that of modern Europe and modern America, the number of ancestors of a single person increases very rapidly, the number of parents being two; of grandparents, four; of great-grandparents, eight; the theoretical number of ancestors twenty generations back would be over a million, or, more accurately, 1,048,576. Twenty generations represent, according to the rate of increase of modern times, about seven hundred years; according to the rate of increase of older times, about four hundred years as a minimum. These figures would apply to the series of generations represented by first-born males; for first-born females the respective numbers would be about five hundred years and three hundred and fifty years. If we consider, however, the actual descent of families, including individuals later born, we might perhaps assume that twenty generations in Europe would represent from eight hundred to nine hundred years, and among primitive peoples perhaps only little less, since in former times the differences between the rapidity of successive generations in Europe and among primitive peoples was not very great. This makes it obvious that it is entirely impossible that as great a number of ancestors as the theory requires can have contributed to the development of the individuals of the present generation. The reason for this is plain. Owing to intermarriages between the same families, large numbers of ancestors will be duplicated in different paternal and maternal lines; and in this way the real ancestry of each individual appears to be much more complex than the purely arithmetical treatment would suggest. The calculation for the ancestor table of the

German Emperor, for instance, is instructive. According to O. Lorenz, the numbers of his ancestors in successive generations were as follows: —

GENERATION	THEORETICAL NUMBER	ACTUAL NUMBER
I	2	2
II	4	4
III	8	8
IV	16	14
V	32	24
VI	64	44
VII	128	74
VIII	256	116*
IX	512	177*
X	1024	256*
XI	2048	342*
XII	4096	533*

A series of forty royal families gives the following averages: —

GENERATION	AVERAGE NUMBER
I	2.00
II	4.00
III	7.75
IV	13.88
V	23.70
VI	40.53

* These generations are not completely known. The values here given are the maximum values which would be found provided the unknown individuals had had no "loss of ancestors."

When we compare these conditions in the thickly popu-lated parts of modern Europe and of America, with their unstable population, with the conditions among primitive tribes, it becomes at once apparent that the total number of ancestors of each type in small communities must be much less than the number of ancestors in the modern states just referred to. A characteristic example is pre-sented by the Eskimo of Smith Sound in North Green-land. From all we know, it seems extremely unlikely that this community ever consisted of more than a few hundred individuals. From what we know about the history of Eskimo communities, we might much rather assume that originally it consisted of a very few families only. The community has been cut off from the outer world for very long periods; and while there may have been accessions of new individuals from outside once each century, on the whole it has remained completely iso-lated. It is therefore obvious that the ancestry of this group cannot contain anything like the million of people required by the theory, but that all the individuals must be interrelated through their remote ancestry.

Considering, now, the laws of inheritance as outlined before, it would appear that in a community of this type, the members of which number little more than two hundred individuals, the ancestor of every single individual from the eighth generation back must have been the same, because the eighth generation would require theoretically two hundred and fifty-six individuals, — a greater number than are actually found in the community; and the occurrence of any individuals who have not a good many near and remote ancestors in common with the whole rest of the community is highly improbable, if not impossible.

It follows from this at once that the variability of the whole series around its typical average must be rather small, because all the members of the group will have a certain amount of family resemblance. This uniformity of type will, of course, be the greater, the more uniform the ancestral group.

On the other hand, these conditions bring about another peculiar characteristic of the isolated group. Owing to the constant recurrence of the same ancestral types among the whole group, the type of the whole people becomes very similar to the characteristic traits of the small ancestral group; and the smaller this group, the stronger will be the probability of the type of the local group being quite distinct from the type of the whole people to which they belong.

It seems to my mind that these conditions explain to a

considerable extent the occurrence of distinct local types in primitive races. When we find, for instance, that in North America a very marked type belongs to the Arctic coast of the continent, that a quite distinct type is found in the Mackenzie basin, still others in well-defined localities on the Pacific coast, again others in the Mississippi basin, one in the southeast, and one along the Rio Grande and in Mexico, — it seems plausible to ascribe their origin to the increase of small isolated groups, which, as we have seen, must necessarily lead to differentiation of type.

This view of the origin of local races is quite in accord with the remarkable results obtained by Johannsen in his studies of heredity. He repeated artificially the conditions which prevail in a small community, and exaggerated them by selecting types of equal form, and by propagating them by self-fertilization. He raised in this way bean-plants from beans of equal weight, and was able to restrict variation of the type, so that practically any kind of bean of particular weight and particular form could be bred true to the type of its ancestor, and without perpetuating the accidental variations of the ancestors. In cases where the ancestry goes back to a limited number of individuals, as among our isolated tribes, the variation will, of course, not be restricted to the same extent; but the characteristic development of a stable type is quite analogous to the experiment made by Johannsen.

Another phenomenon may be pointed out here which is still little investigated, but which deserves careful attention. We have seen that in stable communities in sparsely settled countries the relationship between members of a tribe will be quite close, and that this relationship will necessarily affect the type and its variability. In course of time two areas whose population has thus developed may be thrown into contact, and numerous intermarriages may occur. It will be seen at once, that, although the differences between the two types may be apparently only slight, a complete disturbance in the forms of heredity will result, because a great number of individuals of distinct ancestry are thrown together. To give an example. The South Italians and the Spaniards represent two types not very distinct in physical features, but separated for centuries. The small village communities of Italy, as well as those of Spain, have all the characteristics of communities in which endogamic marriages have been continued for a long period. In the Argentine Republic these two types come into contact and intermarry frequently. We have no observations on the result of this mixture upon physical characteristics, but it has been noted that the distribution of male and female births is quite different from that prevailing in families in which both parents are either Spanish or Italian (Pearl). It is also conceivable that this may be one of the elements bringing about the change of type of urban populations when compared to rural populations in Europe, and that it may have been active in the change of type observed among the descendants of European immigrants in America ; for, although the observations have been made on pure types, in America cases of intermarriages of natives of different villages are much more common than in Europe.

After we have thus considered the influences of heredity and environment, so far as they determine the characteristics of distinct types of man, it remains to add a few words on the individuals constituting each type, and on the different distribution of individuals in distinct types.

I have had to refer repeatedly to the phenomena of variation in the races of man ; and I have pointed out before, that, so far as individual features are concerned, we find that the range of variations in each human type is so great, that overlapping of the range of variation in different types is of constant occurrence. We have seen, for instance, that the medium brains of the Europeans occur with considerable frequency among negroes, and that only the excessively small negro brains have no parallel forms among the Europeans; and correspondingly that the excessively large European brains have no parallel forms among the brains of the negroes. The amount of variability in regard to various physical traits differs very considerably in different races. Most of the European types, for instance, are remarkable for their high variability. The same is true of the Polynesians and of some negro tribes. On the other hand, people like the European Hebrews, and, even more so, the North American Indians, are characterized by, comparatively speaking, much greater uniformity. The amount of variability differs considerably with regard to different physical features. It is, for instance, obvious that the hair-color and hair-form of North Europeans is much more variable than the hair-color and hair-form of the Chinese. In Europe the colors vary from flaxen to black, with a considerable number of individuals with red hair, and the form varies from straight to high degrees of waviness. Among the Chinese, on the other hand, we do not find equal variations in the darkness of color, since blondes and curly-haired individuals are absent. Similar observations may be made in regard to stature, head-form, or any other feature of the body that can be expressed by measurements.

The reason for the differences in variability is partly given in our previous remarks. We have seen, when a people is descended from a small uniform group, that then its variability will decrease; while on the other hand, when a group has a much-varied origin, or when the ancestors belong to entirely distinct types, the variability may be considerably increased. In all cases which have been investigated, even in those in which the variability is small, there still remain considerable differences in bodily appearance among the individuals constituting a tribal or national or other social unit; and what is true of the physical traits is obviously no less true of the mental traits, but it is difficult to express mental characteristics in numerical terms of variability. An acquaintance with tribes which are apparently on the simplest level socially, however, shows the existence of certain individuals of most diverse types of disposition and intellect; and as might be expected, if we consider mental condition as dependent upon bodily form, the great variability, even in the most uniform group, of the structure of the body, particularly of the brain, makes it plausible that very large differences in individual disposition may be expected.

What we have said before in regard to the overlapping of variations among different races and types, and the great range of variability in each type, may also be expressed by saying that the differences between different types of man are, on the whole, small as compared to the range of variation in each type.

The importance of these observations in the domain of mental development will be the subject of our future discussions.

IV. THE MENTAL TRAITS OF PRIMITIVE MAN AND OF CIVILIZED MAN

IN the preceding chapters we have discussed the biological conditions of various races and of different social groups, in so far as they form the basis of mental activity. We must now turn our attention to the psychological characteristics of mankind under the varying conditions of race and environment.

When we consider our problem from a purely psychological point of view, we have to follow out the same lines of thought which we pursued in our discussion of the anatomical problem. We must try to enumerate clearly the typical differences between the human mind and the animal mind, which must serve as the background of our discussions. In the treatment of the psychic differences between civilized man and primitive man, we must distinguish the two problems of differences in cultural state of members of the same race, and differences in characteristics of different races; in other words, the problems of environmental influences and of influences of heredity.

For the purposes of our investigation, we do not need to enter deeply into a discussion of the first-named problem, the differences between the minds of the animal and of man. The differences are so striking that little or no diversity of opinion exists. The two outer traits in which the distinction between the minds of animal and of man finds expression are the existence of organized articulate language in man, and the use of utensils of varied application. Both of these are common to the whole of mankind. No tribe has ever been found that does not possess a well-organized language; no community that does not know the use of instruments for breaking, cutting, or drilling, the use of fire and of weapons with which to defend themselves and to obtain the means of living. Although means of communication by sound exist in animals, and although even lower animals seem to have means of bringing about co-operation between different individuals, we do not know of any case of true articulate language from which the student can extract abstract principles of classification of ideas. It may also be that higher apes employ now and then limbs of trees or stones for defence, but the use of complex utensils is not found in any representative of the animal series. Only in the case of habitations do we find an approach to more complex activities, which, however, remain absolutely stable in each species,— as we say, instinctive, — and bear no evidence of any individual freedom of use, which constitutes the primary character of human inventions. The origin of the instinctive activities of animals which lead to the construction of complex mechanical devices is still a hidden secret; but the relation of the individual of the species to these activities differs from that of man to his inventions in the complete lack of freedom of control.

We are accustomed to say that the essential characteristic of the mental processes of man is the power of reasoning. While animals as well as man may perform actions suited to an end, based on memory of the results of previous actions, and suitable selection of actions fitting a certain purpose, we have no evidence whatever that would show that the abstract concepts accompanying the action can be isolated by animals, while all groups of man, from the most primitive to the most highly developed, possess this faculty.

These few remarks on the common mental traits of man will suffice. When we turn to a consideration of the racial and social characteristics of the human mind, we find ourselves confronted by a peculiar difficulty. In all our thoughts we think in terms of our own social envi-

H

ronment.   But the activities of the human mind exhibit
an infinite variety of form among the peoples of the world.
In order to understand these clearly, the student must endeavor to divest himself entirely of opinions and emotions
based upon the peculiar social environment into which he
is born.   He must adapt his own mind, so far as feasible,
to that of the people whom he is studying.   The more
successful he is in freeing himself from the bias based on
the group of ideas that constitute the civilization in which
he lives, the more successful he will be in interpreting the
beliefs and actions of man.   He must follow lines of
thought that are new to him.   He must participate in
new emotions, and understand how, under unwonted
conditions, both lead to actions.   Beliefs, customs, and
the response of the individual to the events of daily life,
give us ample opportunity to observe the manifestations
of the mind of man under varying conditions.

Apparently the thoughts and actions of civilized man,
and those found in more primitive forms of society, prove,
that, in various groups of mankind, the mind responds
quite differently when exposed to the same conditions.
Lack of logical connection in its conclusions, lack of control of will, are apparently two of its fundamental characteristics in primitive society.   In the formation of opin-

ions, belief takes the place of logical demonstration. The emotional value of opinions is great, and consequently they quickly lead to action. The will appears unbalanced, there being a readiness to yield to strong emotions and a stubborn resistance in trifling matters.

Unfortunately the descriptions of the state of mind of primitive people, such as are given by most travellers, are too superficial to be used for psychological investigation. Very few travellers understand the language of the people they visit; and how is it possible to judge a tribe solely by the descriptions of interpreters, or by observations of disconnected actions the incentive of which remains unknown? But even when the language of the people is known to the visitor, he is generally an unappreciative listener to their tales. The missionary has his strong bias against the religious ideas and customs of primitive people, and the trader has no interest in their beliefs and in their barbarous arts. The observers who seriously tried to enter into the inner life of a people, the Cushings, Callaways, and Greys, are few in number, and may be counted on one's fingers. Nevertheless the bulk of the argument is always based on the statements of hasty and superficial observers.

Numerous attempts have been made to describe the

peculiar psychological characteristics of primitive man. Among these I would mention those of Klemm, Carus, De Gobineau, Nott and Gliddon, Waitz, Spencer, and Tylor. Their investigations are of merit as descriptions of the characteristics of primitive people, but we cannot claim for any of them that they describe the psychological characters of races independent of their social surroundings. Klemm and Wuttke designate the civilized races as active, all others as passive, and assume that all elements and beginnings of civilization found among primitive people — in America or on the islands of the Pacific Ocean — were due to an early contact with civilization. Carus divides mankind into "peoples of the day, night and dawn." De Gobineau calls the yellow race the male element, the black race the female element, and calls only the whites the noble and gifted race. Nott and Gliddon ascribe animal instincts only to the lower races, while they declare that the white race has a higher instinct which incites and directs its development.

The belief in the higher hereditary powers of the white race has gained a new life with the modern doctrine of the prerogatives of the master-mind, which have found their boldest expression in Nietzsche's writings.

All such views are generalizations which either do not

sufficiently take into account the social conditions of races, and thus confound cause and effect, or were dictated by scientific or humanitarian bias, by the desire to justify the institution of slavery, or to give the greatest freedom to the most highly gifted.

Tylor and Spencer, who give an ingenious analysis of the mental life of primitive man, do not assume that these are racial characteristics, although the evolutionary standpoint of Spencer's work often seems to convey this impression.

Quite distinct from these is Waitz's point of view. He says, "According to the current opinion the stage of culture of a people or of an individual is largely or exclusively a product of his faculty. We maintain that the reverse is at least just as true. The faculty of man does not designate anything but how much and what he is able to achieve in the immediate future and depends upon the stages of culture through which he has passed and the one he has reached."

The views of these investigators show that in the domain of psychology a confusion prevails still greater than in anatomy, as to the characteristics of primitive races, and that no clear distinction is drawn between the racial and the social problem. In other words, the evidence is based partly on the supposed mental characteristics of races, no matter what their stage of culture; partly on those of tribes and peoples on different levels of civilization, no matter whether they belong to the same race or to distinct races. Still these two problems are entirely distinct. The former is a problem of heredity; the latter, a problem of environment.

Thus we recognize that there are two possible explanations of the different manifestations of the mind of man. It may be that the minds of different races show differences of organization; that is to say, the laws of mental activity may not be the same for all minds. But it may also be that the organization of mind is practically identical among all races of man; that mental activity follows the same laws everywhere, but that its manifestations depend upon the character of individual experience that is subjected to the action of these laws.

It is quite evident that the activities of the human mind depend upon these two elements. The organization of the mind may be denned as the group of laws which determine the modes of thought and of action, irrespective of the subject-matter of mental activity. Subject to such laws are the manner of discrimination between perceptions, the manner in which perceptions associate themselves with previous perceptions, the manner in which a stimulus leads to action, and the emotions produced by stimuli. These laws determine to a great extent the manifestations of the mind. In these we recognize hereditary causes.

But, on the other hand, the influence of individual experience can easily be shown to be very great. The bulk of the experience of man is gained from oft-repeated impressions. It is one of the fundamental laws of psychology that the repetition of mental processes increases the facility with which these processes are performed, and decreases the degree of consciousness that accompanies them. This law expresses the well-known phenomena of habit. When a certain perception is frequently associated with another previous perception, the one will habitually call forth the other. When a certain stimulus frequently results in a certain action, it will tend to call forth habitually the same action. If a stimulus has often produced a certain emotion, it will tend to reproduce it every time. These belong to the group of environmental causes.

The explanation of the activity of the mind of man, therefore, requires the discussion of two distinct problems. The first bears upon the question of unity or diversity of organization of the mind, while the second bears upon the diversity produced by the variety of contents of the mind as found in the various social and geographical environments.   The task of the investigator consists largely in separating these two causes, and in attributing to each its proper share in the development of the peculiarities of the mind.

We will first devote our attention to the question, Do differences exist in the organization of the human mind ? Since Waitz's thorough discussion of the question of the unity of the human species, there can be no doubt that in the main the mental characteristics of man are the same all over the world; but the question remains open, whether there is a sufficient difference in grade to allow us to assume that the present races of man may be considered as standing on different stages of the evolutionary series, whether we are justified in ascribing to civilized man a higher place in organization than to primitive man.

The chief difficulty encountered in the solution of this problem has been pointed out before. It is the uncertainty as to which of the characteristics of primitive man are causes of the low stage of culture, and which are caused by it; or which of the psychological characteristics are hereditary, and would not be wiped out by the effects of civilization. The fundamental difficulty of collecting satisfactory observations lies in the fact that no large groups of primitive man are brought nowadays into conditions of real equality with whites. The gap between our society and theirs always remains open, and for this reason their minds cannot be expected to work in the same manner as ours. The same phenomenon which led us to the conclusion that primitive races of our times are not given an opportunity to develop their abilities, prevents us from judging their innate faculty.

It seems advantageous to direct our attention first of all to this difficulty. If it can be shown that certain mental traits are common to all members of mankind that are on a primitive stage of civilization, no matter what their racial affinities may be, the conclusion will gain much in strength, that these traits are primarily social, or based on physical characteristics due to social environment.

I will select a few only among the mental characteristics of primitive man which will illustrate our point, — inhibition of impulses, power of attention, power of original thought.

We will first discuss the question, in how far primitive man is capable of inhibiting impulses (Spencer).

It is an impression obtained by many travellers, and also based upon experiences gained in our own country, that primitive man of all races, and the less educated of our own race, have in common a lack of control of emotions, that they give way more readily to an impulse than civilized man and the highly educated. I believe that this conception is based largely upon the neglect to consider the occasions on which a strong control of impulses is demanded in various forms of society.

Most of the proofs for this alleged peculiarity are based on the fickleness and uncertainty of the disposition of primitive man, and on the strength of his passions aroused by seemingly trifling causes. I will say right here that the traveller or student measures the fickleness of the people by the importance which he attributes to the actions or purposes in which they do not persevere, and he weighs the impulse for outbursts of passion by his standard. Let me give an example. A traveller desirous of reaching his goal as soon as possible engages men to start on a journey at a certain time. To him time is exceedingly valuable. But what is time to primitive man, who does not feel the compulsion of completing a definite work at a definite time? While the traveller is fuming and raging over the delay, his men keep up their merry chatter and laughter, and cannot be induced to exert themselves except to please their master. Would not they be right in stigmatizing many a traveller for his impulsiveness and lack of control when irritated by a trifling cause like loss of time? Instead of this, the traveller complains of the fickleness of the natives, who quickly lose interest in the objects which the traveller has at heart.

The proper way to compare the fickleness of the savage and that of the white is to compare their behavior in undertakings which are equally important to each. More generally speaking, when we want to give a true estimate of the power of primitive man to control impulses, we must not compare the control required on certain occasions among ourselves with the control exerted by primitive man on the same occasions. If, for instance, our social etiquette forbids the expression of feelings of personal discomfort and of anxiety, we must remember that personal etiquette among primitive men may not require any inhibition of the same kind. We must rather look for those occasions on which inhibition is required by the customs of primitive man. Such are, for instance, the numerous cases of taboo, — that is, of prohibitions of the use of certain foods, or of the performance of certain kinds of work, — which sometimes require a considerable amount of self-control. When an Eskimo community is on the point of starvation, and their religious proscriptions forbid them to make use of the seals that are basking on the ice, the amount of self-control of the whole community which restrains them from killing these seals is certainly very great. Other examples that suggest themselves are the perseverance of primitive man in the manufacture of his utensils and weapons; his readiness to undergo privations and hardships which promise to fulfil his desires, — as the Indian youth's willingness to fast in the mountains, awaiting the appearance of his guardian spirit; or his bravery and endurance exhibited in order to gain admittance to the ranks of the men of his tribe; or, again, the often-described power of endurance exhibited by Indian captives who undergo torture at the hands of their enemies.

It has also been claimed that lack of control is exhibited by primitive man in his outbursts of passion occasioned by slight provocations. I think that in this case also the difference in attitude of civilized man and of primitive man disappears if we give due weight to the social conditions in which the individual lives.

What would a primitive man say to the noble passion which preceded and accompanied the war of the Rebellion? Would not the rights of slaves seem to him a most irrelevant question? On the other hand, we have ample proof that his passions are just as much controlled as ours, only in different directions. The numerous customs and restrictions regulating the relations of the sexes may serve as an example. The difference in impulsiveness may be fully explained by the different weight of motives in both cases. In short, perseverance and control of impulses are demanded of primitive man as well as of civilized man, but on different occasions. If they are not demanded as often, the cause must be looked for, not in the inherent inability to produce them, but in the social status which does not demand them to the same extent.

Spencer mentions as a particular case of this lack of control the improvidence of primitive man. I believe it would be more proper to say, instead of improvidence, optimism. "Why should I not be as successful to-morrow as I was to-day?" is the underlying feeling of primitive man. This feeling is, I think, no less powerful in civilized man. What builds up business activity but the belief in the stability of existing conditions? Why do the poor not hesitate to found families without being able to lay in store beforehand? We must not forget that starvation among most primitive people is an exceptional case, the same as financial crises among civilized people; and that for times of need, such as occur regularly, provision is always made. Our social status is more stable, so far as the acquiring of the barest necessities of life is concerned, so that exceptional conditions do not prevail often; but nobody would maintain that the majority of civilized men are always prepared to meet emergencies. We may recognize a difference in the degree of improvidence caused by the difference of social status, but not a specific difference between lower and higher types of man.

Related to the lack of power of inhibition is another trait which has been ascribed to primitive man of all races, — his inability of concentration when any demand is made upon the more complex faculties of the intellect. I will mention an example which seems to make clear the error committed in this assumption. In his description of the natives of the west coast of Vancouver Island, Sproat says, "The native mind, to an educated man, seems generally to be asleep. . . . On his attention being fully aroused, he often shows much quickness in

reply and ingenuity in argument. But a short conversation wearies him, particularly if questions are
asked that require efforts of thought or memory on his
part. The mind of the savage then appears to rock to
and fro out of mere weakness." Spencer, who quotes
this passage, adds a number of others corroborating this
point. I happen to know through personal contact the
tribes mentioned by Sproat. The questions put by the
traveller seem mostly trifling to the Indian, and he naturally soon tires of a conversation carried on in a foreign
language, and one in which he finds nothing to interest
him. As a matter of fact, the interest of those natives
can easily be raised to a high pitch, and I have often been
the one who was wearied out first. Neither does the
management of their intricate system of exchange prove
mental inertness in matters which concern the natives.
Without mnemonic aids, they plan the systematic distribution of their property in such a manner as to increase
their wealth and social position. These plans require
great foresight and constant application.

Finally I wish to refer to a trait of the mental life of
primitive man of all races which has often been adduced
as the primary reason why certain races cannot rise to
higher levels of culture ; namely, their lack of originality.

It is said that the conservatism of primitive man is so strong, that the individual never deviates from the traditional customs and beliefs (Spencer). While there is certainly truth in this statement in so far as more customs are binding than in civilized society, at least in its most highly developed types, originality is a trait which is by no means lacking in the life of primitive people. I will call to mind the great frequency of the appearance of prophets among newly converted tribes as well as among pagan tribes. Among the latter we learn quite frequently of new dogmas which have been introduced by such individuals. It is true that these may often be traced to the influence of the ideas of neighboring tribes, but they are modified by the individuality of the person, and grafted upon the current beliefs of the people. It is a well-known fact that myths and beliefs have been disseminated, and undergo changes in the process of dissemination (Boas). Undoubtedly this has often been accomplished by the independent thought of individuals, as may be observed in the increasing complexity of esoteric doctrines intrusted to the care of a priesthood. I believe one of the best examples of such independent thought is furnished by the history of the ghost-dance ceremonies in North America (Mooney). The doctrines of the ghost-dance prophets were new, but based on the ideas of their own people, their neighbors, and the teachings of missionaries. The notion of future life of an Indian tribe of Vancouver Island has undergone a change in this manner, in so far as the idea of the return of the dead in children of their own family has arisen. The same independent attitude may be observed in the replies of the Nicaraguan Indians to the questions regarding their religion as were put to them by Bobadilla, and which were reported by Oviedo.

It seems to my mind that the mental attitude of individuals who thus develop the beliefs of a tribe is exactly that of the civilized philosopher. The student of the history of philosophy is well aware how strongly the mind of even the greatest genius is influenced by the current thought of his time. This has been well expressed by a German writer (Lehmann), who says, "The character of a system of philosophy is, just like that of any other literary work, determined first of all by the personality of its originator. Every true philosophy reflects the life of the philosopher, as well as every true poem that of the poet. Secondly, it bears the general marks of the period to which it belongs; and the more powerful the ideas which it proclaims, the more strongly it will be permeated by the currents of thought which fluctuate in the life of the period. Thirdly, it is influenced by the particular bent of philosophical thought of the period."

If such is the case among the greatest minds of all times, why should we wonder that the thinker in primitive society is strongly influenced by the current thought of his time? Unconscious and conscious imitation are factors influencing civilized society, not less than primitive society, as has been shown by G. Tarde, who has proved that primitive man, and civilized man as well, imitates not such actions only as are useful, and for the imitation of which logical causes may be given, but also others for the adoption or preservation of which no logical reason can be assigned.

I think these considerations illustrate that the differences between civilized man and primitive man are in many cases more apparent than real; that the social conditions, on account of their peculiar characteristics, easily convey the impression that the mind of primitive man acts in a way quite different from ours, while in reality the fundamental traits of the mind are the same.

This does not mean that no differences exist or can be found, only that the method of investigation must be different. It does not seem probable that the minds of races which show variations in their anatomical structure should act in exactly the same manner. Differences of structure must be accompanied by differences of function, physiological as well as psychological; and, as we found clear evidence of difference in structure between the races, so we must anticipate that differences in mental characteristics will be found. Thus, a smaller size or lesser number of nervous elements would probably entail loss of mental energy, and paucity of connections in the central nervous system would produce sluggishness of the mind. As stated before, it seems probable that some slight differences of this character will be found between the white and the negro, for instance, but they have not yet been proved. As all structural differences are quantitative, we must expect to find mental differences to be of the same description; and as we found the variations in structure to overlap, so that many forms are common to individuals of all races, so we may expect that many individuals will not differ in regard to their faculty, while a statistical inquiry embracing whole races would reveal certain differences. Furthermore, as certain anatomical traits are found to be hereditary in certain families, and hence in tribes, and perhaps even in peoples, in the same manner mental traits characterize certain families, and may prevail among tribes. It seems, however, an impossible undertaking to separate in a satisfactory manner the social and the hereditary features. Galton's attempt to establish the laws of hereditary genius, and later endeavors in the same direction, point out a way of treatment for these questions which will prove useful in so far as it opens a method of determining the influence of heredity upon mental qualities.

After we have thus found that the alleged specific differences between civilized and primitive man, so far as they are inferred from complex psychic responses, can be reduced to the same fundamental psychical forms, we have the right to decline as unprofitable a discussion of the hereditary mental traits of various branches of the white race.   Much has been said of the hereditary characteristics of the Jews, of the Gypsies, of the French and Irish, but I do not see that the external and social causes which have moulded the character of members of these people have ever been eliminated satisfactorily; and, moreover, I do not see how this can be accomplished.   A number of external factors that influence body and mind may easily be named, — climate, nutrition, occupation, – but as soon as we enter into a consideration of social factors and mental conditions, we are unable to tell definitely what is cause and what is effect.   An appar-

ently excellent discussion of external influences upon the
character of a people has been given by A. Wernich in his
description of the character of the Japanese. He finds
some of their peculiarities caused by the lack of vigor of
the muscular and alimentary systems, which in their turn
are due to improper nutrition; while he recognizes as hereditary other physiological traits which influence the mind.
And still, how weak appear his conclusions, after the
energy and endurance exhibited by the Japanese in their
modern development and in their conflict with Russia !

Effects of malnutrition continued through many generations might be expected to affect the mental life of
the Bushmen and the Lapps (Virchow) ; and still, after
the experience just quoted, we may well hesitate before we
express any definite conclusions.

It would seem, therefore, that we have no right to
explain difference in mental attitude of different groups
of people, particularly of closely related ones, as due to
hereditary causes, until we have been able to prove that
physiological and the correlated psychological traits are
hereditary, regardless of social and natural environment.

A beginning in work of this kind has been made in the
experimental investigations of school-children in regard
to simple mental activities and simple physiological pro-

cesses; in the work of the Cambridge Scientific Expedition to Torres Strait (Rivers), in which the first systematic attempt has been made to study the simple psychical reactions of primitive people; and in the investigations carried on systematically by Dr. Woodworth on the primitive people exhibited at the World's Fair of St. Louis. Up to this time the results are, on the whole, not favorable to the theory of the occurrence of very fundamental differences between different races.

One additional point of our inquiry into the organic basis of mental activity remains to be investigated; namely, the question, Has the organic basis for the faculty of man been improved by civilization, and particularly may that of primitive races be improved by this agency? We must consider both the anatomical and the psychological aspects of this question. I have already pointed out that civilization causes anatomical changes of the same description as those accompanying the domestication of animals. It is likely that changes of mental character go hand in hand with them. The observed anatomical changes are, however, limited to this group of phenomena. We cannot prove that any progressive changes of the human organism have taken place; and particularly no advance in the size or complexity of the structure of the central nervous system, caused by the cumulative effects of civilization, can be proved.

The difficulty of proving a progress of faculty is still greater. It seems to me that the probable effect of civilization upon an evolution of human faculty has been much overestimated. The psychical changes which are the immediate consequence of domestication or civilization may be considerable. They are changes due to the influence of environment. It is doubtful, however, if any progressive changes, or such as are transmitted by heredity, have taken place. The number of generations subjected to this influence seems altogether too small. For large portions of Europe we cannot assume more than forty or fifty generations; and even this number is probably considerably too high, inasmuch as in the middle ages the bulk of the population lived on very low stages of civilization.

Besides this, the tendency of human multiplication is such, that the most highly cultured families tend to disappear, while others which have been less subjected to the influences regulating the life of the most cultured class take their place. Therefore it is much less likely that advance is hereditary than that it is transmitted by means of education.

In illustrating the improving effects of civilization through transmission, much weight is generally laid upon cases of relapse of individuals belonging to primitive races who have been educated. These relapses are interpreted as proofs of the inability of the child of a lower race to adapt itself to our high civilization, even if the best advantages are given to it. It is true that a considerable number of such cases are on record. Among these I will mention Darwin's Fuegian, who lived in England for a few years and returned to his home, where he fell back into the ways of his primitive countrymen; and the West Australian girl who was married to a white man, but suddenly fled to the bush after killing her husband, and resumed life with the natives. Cases of this kind are true, but not one of them has been described with sufficient detail. The social and mental conditions of the individual have never been subjected to a searching analysis. I should judge that even in extreme cases, notwithstanding their better education, their social position was always one of isolation, while the ties of consanguinity formed a connecting link with their uncivilized brethren. The power with which society holds us and does not give us a chance to step out of its limits cannot have acted as strongly upon them as upon us. On the other hand, the station obtained by many negroes in our civilization seems to me to have just as much weight as the few cases of relapse which have been collected with much care and diligence. I should place side by side with them the cases of white men who live alone among native tribes, and who sink almost invariably to a semi-barbarous position, and the members of well-to-do families who prefer unbounded freedom to the fetters of society, and flee to the wilderness, where many lead a life in no way superior to that of primitive man.

In the study of the behavior of members of foreign races educated in European society, we should also bear in mind the influence of habits of thought, feeling, and action acquired in early childhood, and of which no recollection is retained. If S. Freud is right in assuming that these forgotten incidents remain a living force throughout life, — the more potent, the more thoroughly they are forgotten, — we should have to conclude that many of the small traits of individuals which we ordinarily believe to be inherited are acquired by the influence of the individuals among whom the child spends the first five years of its life. All observations on the force of habit and the intensity of resistance to changes of habit are in favor of this theory.

Our brief consideration of some of the mental activities of man in civilized and in primitive society has led us to the conclusion that these functions of the human mind are common to the whole of humanity. It may be well to state here, that, according to our present method of considering biological and psychological phenomena, we must assume that these have developed from lower conditions existing at a previous time, and that at one time there certainly must have been races and tribes in which the properties here described were not at all, or only slightly, developed; but it is also true that among the present races of man, no matter how primitive they may be in comparison with ourselves, these faculties are highly developed.

It is not impossible that the degree of development of these functions may differ somewhat among different types of man; but I do not believe that we are able at the present time to form a just valuation of the hereditary mental powers of the different races. A comparison of their languages, customs, and activities suggests that their faculties may be unequally developed; but the differences are not sufficient to justify us to ascribe materially lower stages to some peoples, and higher stages to others. The conclusions reached from these considerations are therefore, on the whole, negative. We are not inclined to consider the mental organization of different races of man as differing in fundamental points. Although, therefore, the distribution of faculty among the races of man is far from being known, we can say this much : the average faculty of the white race is found to the same degree in a large proportion of individuals of all other races, and, although it is probable that some of these races may not produce as large a proportion of great men as our own race, there is no reason to suppose that they are unable to reach the level of civilization represented by the bulk of our own people.

V. RACE AND LANGUAGE

In the last chapter I tried to show that the principal characteristics of the mind of primitive man occur among primitive tribes of all races, and that therefore the inference must not be drawn that these traits of the mind are racial characteristics. This negative conclusion, which is based entirely on the consideration of a few selected points that occur with great regularity in the description of primitive tribes, does not give us, however, proof positive of the lack of all correlation between mental life and racial descent, and we must direct our attention to those cases in which an immediate relationship between the two may be and has been claimed.

This has occurred particularly in regard to language and racial types. Indeed, the opinion is still held by some investigators that linguistic relationships and racial relationships are in a way interchangeable terms. An example illustrating this point of view may be seen in the long-continued discussions of the home of the "Aryan race," in which the blond northwest European type is identified with the ancient people among whom the Indo-European or Aryan languages developed.

If it could be shown that distinct languages belong to distinct racial types, and that these languages exhibit different levels of development or indicate different types of thought, we should have gained a sound basis which would allow us to discuss the genius of each people as reflected in its language   If, furthermore, we could show that certain cultural types belong to certain races and are foreign to the genius of others, our conclusions would be founded on much firmer ground.

Thus we are led to a consideration of the all-important question whether types, languages, and cultures are so intimately connected that each human race is characterized by a certain combination of physical type, language, and culture.

It is obvious, that, if this correlation should exist in a strict sense, attempts to classify mankind from any one of the three points of view would necessarily lead to the same results; in other words, each point of view could be used independently or in combination with the other ones, to study the relations between the different groups of mankind. As a matter of fact, attempts of this kind have often been made. A number of classifications of the

races of man are based wholly on anatomical characteristics, yet often combined with geographical considerations; others are based on the discussion of a combination of anatomical and cultural traits which are
considered as characteristic of certain groups of mankind; while still others are based primarily on the
study of the languages spoken by people representing a
certain anatomical type.

The attempts that have thus been made have led to
entirely different results (Topinard). Blumenbach, one
of the first scientists who attempted to classify mankind,
distinguished five races, — the Caucasian, Mongolian,
Ethiopian, American, and Malay. It is fairly clear that
this classification is based as much on geographical as on
anatomical considerations, although the description of
each race is primarily an anatomical one. Cuvier distinguished three races, — the white, yellow, and black.
Huxley proceeded more strictly on a biological basis.
He combined part of the Mongolian and American races
of Blumenbach into one, assigned part of the South Asiatic peoples to the Australian type, and subdivided the
European race into a dark and a light division. The numerical preponderance of the European types evidently
led him to make finer distinctions in this race, which he

divided into the xanthochroic or blond, and melano-chroic or dark races. It would be easy to make subdivisions of equal value in other races. Still clearer is the influence of cultural points of view in classifications like those of Gobineau and of Klemm, the latter of whom distinguished the active and passive races according to the cultural achievements of the various types of man.

The most typical attempt to classify mankind from a consideration of both anatomical and linguistic points of view is that of Friedrich Müller, who takes as the basis of his primary divisions the form of hair, while all the minor divisions are based on linguistic considerations.

An attempt to correlate the numerous classifications that have been proposed shows clearly a condition of utter confusion and contradiction; so that we are led to the conclusion that type, language, and type of culture, may not be closely and permanently connected. We must therefore consider the actual development of these various traits among the existing races.

At the present period we may observe many cases in which a complete change of language and culture takes place without a corresponding change in physical type. This is true, for instance, among the North American negroes, a people by descent largely African; in culture and language, however, essentially European. While it is true that certain survivals of African culture and language are found among our American negroes, their culture is essentially that of the uneducated classes of the people among whom they live, and their language is on the whole identical with that of their neighbors, — English, French, Spanish, and Portuguese, according to the prevalent language in various parts of the continent. It might be objected that the transportation of the African race to America was an artificial one, and that in earlier times extended migrations and transplantations of this kind have not taken place.

The history of mediæval Europe, however, demonstrates that extended changes in language and culture have taken place many times without corresponding changes in blood.

Recent investigations of the physical types of Europe have shown with great clearness that the distribution of types has remained the same for a long period. Without considering details, it may be said that an Alpine type can easily be distinguished from a North European type on the one hand, and a South European type on the other (Ripley). The Alpine type appears fairly uniform over a large territory, no matter what language may be spoken

and what national culture may prevail in the particular district. The Central European Frenchmen, Germans, Italians, and Slavs are so nearly of the same
type, that we may safely assume a considerable degree
of blood-relationship, notwithstanding their linguistic
differences.

Instances of similar kind, in which we find permanence
of blood with far-reaching modifications of language and
culture, are found in other parts of the world. As an example may be mentioned the Veddah of Ceylon, a people
fundamentally different in type from the neighboring
Singhalese, whose language they seem to have adopted,
and from whom they have also evidently borrowed a
number of cultural traits (Sarasin). Still other examples
are the Japanese of the northern part of Japan, who are
undoubtedly, to a considerable extent, Ainu in blood
(Balz); and the Yukaghir of Siberia, who, while retaining to a great extent the old blood, have been assimilated
in culture and language by the neighboring Tungus
(Jochelson).

While it is therefore evident that in many cases a people,
without undergoing a considerable change in type by
mixture, has changed completely its language and culture, still other cases may be adduced in which it can be

shown that a people has retained its language while undergoing material changes in blood and culture, or in both. As an example of this may be mentioned the Magyar of Europe, who have retained their old language, but have become mixed with people speaking Indo-European languages, and who have, to all intents and purposes, adopted European culture.

Similar conditions must have prevailed among the Athapascans, one of the great linguistic families of North America. The great body of people speaking languages belonging to this linguistic stock live in the northwestern part of America, while other dialects are spoken by small tribes in California, and still others by a large body of people in Arizona and New Mexico.[1] The relationship between all these dialects is so close that they must be considered as branches of one large group, and it must be assumed that all of them have sprung from a language once spoken over a continuous area. At the present time the people speaking these languages differ fundamentally in type, the inhabitants of the Mackenzie River region being quite different from the tribes of California, and these, again, differing from the tribes of New Mexico

[1] See map in Handbook of American Indians (Bulletin 30 of the Bureau of American Ethnology), part i (1907).

(Boas). The forms of culture in these different regions are also quite distinct : the culture of the California Athapascans resembles that of other Californian tribes, while the culture of the Athapascans of New Mexico and Arizona is influenced by that of other peoples of that area (Goddard). It seems most plausible to assume in this case that branches of this stock migrated from one part of this large area to another, where they intermingled with the neighboring people, and thus changed their physical characteristics, while at the same time they retained their speech. Without historical evidence, this process cannot, of course, be proved.

These two phenomena, — retention of type with change of language, and retention of language with change of type, — apparently opposed to each other, are still very closely related, and in many cases go hand in hand. An example of this is, for instance, the distribution of the Arabs along the north coast of Africa. On the whole, the Arab element has retained its language ; but at the same time intermarriages with the native races were common, so that the descendants of the Arabs have often retained their old language, and have changed their type. On the other hand, the natives have to a certain extent given up their own languages, but have continued to intermarry among themselves, and have thus preserved their type. So far as any change of this kind is connected with intermixture, both types of changes must always occur at the same time, and will be classed as a change of type or a change of language, as our attention is directed to the one people or the other, or, in some cases, as the one or the other change is more pronounced. Cases of complete assimilation without any mixture of the people involved seem to be rare, if not entirely absent.

Cases of permanence of type and language and of change of culture are much more numerous. As a matter of fact, the whole historical development of Europe, from prehistoric times on, is one endless series of examples of this process, which seems to be much easier, since assimilation of cultures occurs everywhere without actual blood-mixture, as an effect of imitation. Proof of diffusion of cultural elements may be found in every single cultural area which covers a district in which many languages are spoken. In North America, California offers a good example of this kind; for here many languages are spoken, and there is a certain degree of differentiation of type, but at the same time a considerable uniformity of culture prevails (Kroeber). Another case in point is the coast of New Guinea, where, notwithstanding strong local differentiations, a certain fairly characteristic type of culture prevails, which goes hand in hand with a strong differentiation of languages. Among more highly civilized peoples, the whole area which is under the influence of Chinese culture might be given as an example.

These considerations make it fairly clear that, at least at the present time, anatomical type, language, and culture have not necessarily the same fates; that a people may remain constant in type and language, and change in culture; that it may remain constant in type, but change in language; or that it may remain constant in language, and change in type and culture. It is obvious, therefore, that attempts to classify mankind, based on the present distribution of type, language, and culture, must lead to different results, according to the point of view taken; that a classification based primarily on type alone will lead to a system which represents more or less accurately the blood-relationships of the people, which do not need to coincide with their cultural relationships; and that in the same way classifications based on language and culture do not need at all to coincide with a biological classification.

If this be true, then a problem like the Aryan problem, to which I referred before, really does not exist, because the problem is primarily a linguistic one, relating to the history of the Aryan languages; and the assumption that a certain definite people whose members have always been related by blood must have been the carriers of this language throughout history, and the other assumption, that a certain cultural type must have always belonged to this people, — are purely arbitrary ones, and not in accord with the observed facts.

Nevertheless it must be granted that in a theoretical consideration of the history of the types of mankind, of languages, and of cultures, we are led back to the assumption of early conditions, during which each type was much more isolated from the rest of mankind than it is at the present time. For this reason the culture and the language belonging to a single type must have been much more sharply separated from those of other types than we find them to be at the present period. It is true that such a condition has nowhere been observed; but the knowledge of historical developments almost compels us to assume its existence at a very early period in the development of mankind. If this is true, the question would arise, whether an isolated group at an early period was necessarily characterized by a single type, a single language, and a single culture, or whether in such a group

different types, different languages, and different cultures
may have been represented.

The historical development of mankind would afford a
simpler and clearer picture if we were justified in assuming that in primitive communities the three phenomena
had been intimately associated. No proof, however, of
such an assumption, can be given. On the contrary, the
present distribution of languages, as compared with the
distribution of types, makes it plausible that even at the
earliest times the biological units may have been wider
than the linguistic units, and presumably also wider than
the cultural units. I believe it may be safely said that all
over the world the biological unit — disregarding
minute local differences — is much larger than the linguistic unit; in other words, that groups of men who are
so closely related in bodily appearance that we must consider them as representatives of the same variety of mankind, embrace a much larger number of individuals than
the number of men speaking languages which we know to
be genetically related. Examples of this kind may be
given from many parts of the world. Thus, the European race — including under this term roughly all those
individuals who are without hesitation classed by us as
members of the white race — would include peoples

speaking Indo-European, Basque, and Ural-Altaic languages. West African Negroes would represent individuals
of a certain Negro type, but speaking the most diverse
languages; and the same would be true, among Asiatic
types, of Siberians; among American types, of part of
the Californian Indians.

So far as our historical evidence goes, there is no reason
to believe that the number of distinct languages has at any
time been less than it is now. On the contrary, all our
evidence goes to show that the number of apparently
unrelated languages was much greater in earlier times
than at present. On the other hand, the number of types
that have presumably become extinct seems to be rather
small, so that there is no reason to suppose that at an
early period there should have been a nearer correspond-
ence between the number of distinct linguistic and anatomical types; and we are thus led to the conclusion that
presumably at an early time each human type may have
existed in a number of small isolated groups, each of
which may have possessed a language and culture of its
own.

Incidentally we may remark here, that, from this point
of view, the great diversity of languages found in many
remote mountain areas should not be explained as the

result of a gradual pressing-back of remnants of tribes into inaccessible districts, but appears rather as a survival of an older general condition of mankind, when every continent was inhabited by smaller groups of people speaking distinct languages. The present conditions would have developed through the gradual extinction of many of the old stocks and their absorption or extinction by others, which thus came to occupy a more extended territory.

However this may be, the probabilities are decidedly in favor of the assumption that there is no necessity to assume that originally each language and culture were confined to a single type, or that each type and culture were confined to one language; in short, that there has been at any time a close correlation between these three phenomena.

The assumption that type, language, and culture were originally closely correlated would entail the further assumption that these three traits developed approximately at the same period, and that they developed conjointly for a considerable length of time. This assumption does not seem by any means plausible. The fundamental types of man which are represented in the Negroid race and in the Mongoloid race must have been differentiated

long before the formation of those forms of speech that
are now recognized in the linguistic families of the world.
I think that even the differentiation of the more important subdivisions of the great races antedates the formation of the existing linguistic families.   At any rate, the
biological differentiation and the formation of speech
were, at this early period, subject to the same causes that
are acting upon them now, and our whole experience
shows that these causes may bring about great changes in
language much more rapidly than in the human body.
In this consideration lies the principal reason for the
theory of lack of correlation of type and language, even
during the period of formation of types and of linguistic
families.[1]

What is true of language is obviously even more true
of culture.   In other words, if a certain type of man
migrated over a considerable area before its language
assumed the form which can now be traced in related linguistic groups, and before its culture assumed the definite
type the further development of which can now be recog-

[1] This must not be understood to mean that every primitive language
is in a constant state of rapid modification.   There are many evidences
of a great permanence of languages.   When, however, owing to certain
outer or inner causes, changes set in, they are apt to bring about a
thorough modification of the form of speech.

nized, there would be no possibility of ever discovering a correlation of type, language, and culture, even if it had ever existed ; but it is quite possible that such correlation has really never occurred.

It is quite conceivable that a certain racial type may have scattered over a considerable area during a formative period of speech, and that the languages which developed among the various groups of this racial type came to be so different that it is now impossible to prove them to be genetically related. In the same way, new developments of culture may have taken place which are so entirely disconnected with older types that the older genetic relationships, even if they existed, can no longer be discovered.

If we adopt this point of view, and thus eliminate the hypothetical assumption of correlation between primitive type, primitive language, and primitive culture, we recognize that any attempt at classification which includes more than one of these traits cannot be consistent.

It may be added that the general term "culture," which has been used here, may be subdivided from a considerable number of points of view ; and different results again might be expected when we consider the inventions, the types of social organization, or beliefs, as leading points of view in our classification.

After we have thus shown that language, culture, and type cannot be considered as constantly associated, and after we have recognized that the same type of man has developed distinct languages, the question still remains open, whether the languages developed by any one stock bear marks of superiority or inferiority. It has been claimed, for instance, that the highly developed inflected languages of Europe are much superior to the cumbersome agglutinative or polysynthetic languages of northern Asia and of America (Gabelentz). We have also been told that lack of phonetic discrimination, lack of power of abstraction, are characteristics of primitive languages. It is important to show whether these traits are really associated with any languages of primitive man. In a way this consideration leads us back to the study of alleged mental characteristics of distinct human types.

The view of the lack of phonetic differentiation is based on the fact that certain sounds of primitive languages are interpreted by the European sometimes as one of our familiar sounds, sometimes as another; they have been called alternating sounds. A better knowledge of phonetics has shown in all these cases, however, that the sounds are quite definite, but that owing to the manner of their production they are intermediate between sounds familiar to us. Thus an *m* produced by a very weak closing of the lips, and with half-open nose, sounds to our ear a little like *m*, a little like *b*, and a little like *w*; and according to slight accidental changes, it is sometimes heard as one of these sounds, sometimes as another, without, however, being in reality more variable than our *m*. Cases of this kind are quite numerous, but it would be a misinterpretation to adduce them as proof of lack of definiteness of the sound of primitive languages (Boas). In fact, it would seem that limitation in the number of sounds is necessary in each language in order to make possible rapid communication. If the number of sounds that are used in any particular language were unlimited, the accuracy with which the movements of the complicated mechanism required for producing the sounds are performed, would presumably be lacking; and consequently rapidity and accuracy of pronunciation, and with them the possibility of accurate interpretation of the sounds heard, would be difficult or even impossible. On the other hand, limitation of the number of sounds brings it about that the movements required in the production of each become automatic; that the association between the sound heard and the muscular movements, and that between the auditory impression and the muscular sensation of the articulation, become firmly fixed. Thus it would seem that limited phonetic resources are necessary for easy communication.

The second point that is often brought up to characterize primitive languages is the lack of power of classification and abstraction. Here, again, we are easily misled by our habit of using the classifications of our own language, and considering these, therefore, as the most natural ones, and by overlooking the principles of classification used in the languages of primitive people.

It may be well to make clear to our minds what constitutes the elements of all languages. It is a fundamental and common trait of articulate speech that the groups of sounds which are uttered serve to convey ideas, and each group of sounds has a fixed meaning. Languages differ not only in the character of their constituent phonetic elements and sound clusters, but also in the groups of ideas that find expression in fixed phonetic groups.

The total number of possible combinations of phonetic elements is also unlimited, but only a limited number are used to express ideas. This implies that the total number of ideas that are expressed by distinct phonetic groups is limited in number. We will call these phonetic groups "word-stems."

Since the total range of personal experience which language serves to express is infinitely varied, and its whole scope must be expressed by a limited number of word-stems, it is obvious that an extended classification of experiences must underlie all articulate speech.

This coincides with a fundamental trait of human thought. In our actual experience no two sense-impressions or emotional states are identical. Nevertheless we classify them, according to their similarities, in wider or narrower groups, the limits of which may be determined from a variety of points of view. Notwithstanding their individual differences, we recognize in our experiences common elements, and consider them as related or even as the same, provided a sufficient number of characteristic traits belong to them in common. Thus the limitation of the number of phonetic groups expressing distinct ideas is an expression of the psychological fact that many different individual experiences appear to us as representatives of the same category of thought.

As an instance we may mention the color terms of different languages. Although the number of shades of color that may be distinguished is very great, only a small number are designated by special terms. The number of these terms has considerably increased in

recent times. In many primitive languages the groupings of yellow, green, and blue do not agree with ours.
Often yellow and the yellowish-greens are combined in
one group; green and blue, in another. The typical
feature which occurs everywhere is the use of one term
for a large group of similar sensations.

This trait of human thought and speech may be compared in a certain manner to the limitation of the whole
series of possible articulating movements by selection of a
limited number of habitual movements. If the whole
mass of concepts, with all their variants, were expressed
in language by entirely heterogeneous and unrelated
sound-complexes or word-stems, a condition would arise
in which closely related ideas would not show their
relationship by the corresponding relationship of their
sound-symbols, and an infinitely large number of distinct
word-stems would be required for expression. If this
were the case, the association between an idea and its
representative word-stem would not become sufficiently
stable to be reproduced automatically without reflection
at any given moment. In the same way as the automatic
and rapid use of articulations has brought it about that
a limited number of articulations only, each with limited
variability, and a limited number of sound-clusters, have

been selected from the infinitely large range of possible articulations and clusters of articulations, so the infinitely large number of ideas have been reduced by classification to a lesser number, which by constant use have established firm associations, and which can be used automatically.

It seems important at this point of our considerations to emphasize the fact that the groups of ideas expressed by specific word-stems show very material differences in different languages, and do not conform by any means to the same principles of classification. To take the example of English, we find that the idea of "water" is expressed in a great variety of forms: one term serves to express water as a liquid; another one, water in the form of a large expanse (lake); others, water as running in a large body or in a small body (river and brook); still other terms express water in the form of rain, dew, wave, and foam. It is perfectly conceivable that this variety of ideas, each of which is expressed by a single independent term in English, might be expressed in other languages by derivations from the same term.

Another example of the same kind, the words for "snow" in Eskimo, may be given. Here we find one word expressing "snow on the ground;" another one,

L

"falling snow;" a third one, "drifting snow;" a fourth one, "a snowdrift."

In the same language the seal in different conditions is expressed by a variety of terms. One word is the general term for "seal;" another one signifies the "seal basking in the sun;" a third one, a "seal floating on a piece of ice;" not to mention the many names for the seals of different ages and for male and female.

As an example of the manner in which terms that we express by independent words are grouped together under one concept, the Dakota language may be selected. The terms "to kick," "to tie in bundles," "to bite," "to be near to," "to pound," are all derived from the common element meaning "to grip," which holds them together, while we use distinct words for expressing the various ideas.

It seems fairly evident that the selection of such simple terms must to a certain extent depend upon the chief interests of a people; and where it is necessary to distinguish a certain phenomenon in many aspects, which in the life of the people play each an entirely independent role, many independent words may develop, while in other cases modifications of a single term may suffice.

Thus it happens that each language, from the point of

view of another language, may be arbitrary in its classifications; that what appears as a single simple idea in one language may be characterized by a series of distinct word-stems in another.

The tendency of a language to express a complex idea by a single term has been styled "holophrasis" (Powell), and it appears therefore that every language may be holophrastic from the point of view of another language. Holophrasis can hardly be taken as a fundamental characteristic of primitive languages.

We have seen before that some kind of classification of expression must be found in every language. This classification of ideas into groups, each of which is expressed by an independent word-stem, makes it necessary that concepts which are not readily rendered by a single stem should be expressed by combinations or by modifications of the elementary stems in accordance with the elementary ideas to which the particular idea is reduced.

This classification, and the necessity of expressing certain experiences by means of other related ones, — which, by limiting one another, define the special idea to be expressed,— entail the presence of certain formal elements which determine the relations of the single word-stems. If each idea could be expressed by a single word-stem, languages without form would be possible. Since, however, ideas must be expressed by being reduced to a number of related ideas, the kinds of relation become important elements in articulate speech ; and it follows that all languages must contain formal elements, and that their number must be the greater, the less the number of elementary word-stems that define special ideas. In a language which commands a very large, fixed vocabulary, the number of formal elements may become quite small.

After we have thus seen that all languages require and contain certain classifications and formal elements, we will turn to a consideration of the relation between language and thought. It has been claimed that the conciseness and clearness of thought of a people depend to a great extent upon their language. The ease with which in our modern European languages we express wide abstract ideas by a single term, and the facility with which wide generalizations are cast into the frame of a simple sentence, have been claimed to be one of the fundamental conditions of the clearness of our concepts, the logical force of our thought, and the precision with which we eliminate in our thoughts irrelevant details. Apparently this view has much in its favor. When we compare modern English with some of those Indian languages which are most concrete in their formative expression, the contrast is striking. When we say, "The eye is the organ of sight," the Indian may not be able to form the expression "the eye," but may have to define that the eye of a person or of an animal is meant. Neither may the Indian be able to generalize readily the abstract idea of an eye as the representative of the whole class of objects, but may have to specialize by an expression like "this eye here." Neither may he be able to express by a single term the idea of "organ," but may have to specify it by an expression like "instrument of seeing," so that the whole sentence might assume a form like "an indefinite person's eye is his means of seeing." Still it will be recognized that in this more specific form the general idea may be well expressed. It seems very questionable in how far the restriction of the use of certain grammatical forms can really be conceived as a hindrance in the formulation of generalized ideas. It seems much more likely that the lack of these forms is due to the lack of their need. Primitive man, when conversing with his fellow-man, is not in the habit of discussing abstract ideas. His interests centre around the occupations of his daily life; and where philosophic problems are touched upon, they appear either in relation to definite individuals or in the more or less anthropomorphic forms of religious beliefs. Discourses on qualities without connection with the object to which the qualities belong, or of activities or states disconnected from the idea of the actor or the subject being in a certain state, will hardly occur in primitive speech. Thus the Indian will not speak of goodness as such, although he may very well speak of the goodness of a person. He will not speak of a state of bliss apart from the person who is in such a state. He will not refer to the power of seeing without designating an individual who has such power. Thus it happens that in languages in which the idea of possession is expressed by elements subordinated to nouns, all abstract terms appear always with possessive elements. It is, however, perfectly conceivable that an Indian trained in philosophic thought would proceed to free the underlying nominal forms from the possessive elements, and thus reach abstract forms strictly corresponding to the abstract forms of our modern languages. I have made this experiment, for instance, in one of the languages of Vancouver Island, in which no abstract term ever occurs without its possessive elements. After some discussion, I found it perfectly easy to develop the idea of the abstract term in the mind of the Indian, who stated that the word without a possessive

pronoun gives good sense, although it is not used idio-
matically. I succeeded, for instance, in this manner, in
isolating the terms for "love" and "pity," which ordinarily occur only in possessive forms, like "his love for
him" or "my pity for you." That this view is correct,
may also be observed in languages in which possessive
elements appear as independent forms; as, for instance,
in the Siouan languages. In these, pure abstract terms
are quite common.

There is also evidence that other specializing elements,
which are so characteristic of many Indian languages,
may be dispensed with when, for one reason or another, it
seems desirable to generalize a term. To use an example
of a western language,[1] the idea "to be seated" is almost always expressed with an inseparable suffix expressing the place in which a person is seated, as "seated
on the floor of the house, on the ground, on the beach, on
a pile of things," or "on a round thing," etc. When,
however, for some reason, the idea of the state of sitting
is to be emphasized, a form may be used which expresses
simply "being in a sitting posture." In this case, also,
the device for generalized expression is present; but the
opportunity for its application arises seldom, or perhaps

[1] The Kwakiutl of Vancouver Island.

never.   I think what is true in these cases is true of the structure of every single language.   The fact that generalized forms of expression are not used, does not prove inability to form them, but it merely proves that the mode of life of the people is such that they are not required; that they would, however, develop just as soon as needed.

This point of view is also corroborated by a study of the numeral systems of primitive languages.   As is well known, many languages exist in which the numerals do not exceed two or three.   It has been inferred from this that the people speaking these languages are not capable of forming the concept of higher numbers.   I think this interpretation of the existing conditions is quite erroneous.   People like the South American Indians (among whom these defective numeral systems are found), or like the Eskimo (whose old system of numbers probably did not exceed ten), are presumably not in need of higher numerical expressions, because there are not many objects that they have to count.   On the other hand, just as soon as these same people find themselves in contact with civilization, and when they acquire standards of value that have to be counted, they adopt with perfect ease higher numerals from other languages, and develop a more or less perfect system of counting.

This does not mean that every individual who in the course of his life has never made use of higher numerals would acquire more complex systems readily; but the tribe as a whole seems always to be capable of adjusting itself to the needs of counting. It must be borne in mind that counting does not become necessary until objects are considered in such generalized form that their individualities are entirely lost sight of. For this reason it is possible that even a person who owns a herd of domesticated animals may know them by name and by their characteristics, without ever desiring to count them. Members of a war expedition may be known by name, and may not be counted. In short, there is no proof that the lack of the use of numerals is in any way connected with the inability to form the concepts of higher numbers when needed.

If we want to form a correct judgment of the influence that language exerts over thought, we ought to bear in mind that our European languages, as found at the present time, have been moulded to a great extent by the abstract thought of philosophers. Terms like "essence" and "existence," many of which are now commonly used, are by origin artificial devices for expressing the results of abstract thought. In this way they would resemble the artificial, unidiomatic abstract terms that may be formed in primitive languages.

Thus it would seem that the obstacles to generalized thought inherent in the form of a language are of minor importance only, and that presumably language alone would not prevent a people from advancing to more generalized forms of thinking, if the general state of their culture should require expression of such thought; that under these conditions, the language would be moulded rather by the cultural state. It does not seem likely, therefore, that there is any direct relation between the culture of a tribe and the language they speak, except in so far as the form of the language will be moulded by the state of culture, but not in so far as a certain state of culture is conditioned by morphological traits of the language.

Thus we have found that language does not furnish the much-looked-for means of discovering differences in the mental status of different races.

VI. THE UNIVERSALITY OF CULTURAL TRAITS

THERE remains one question to be discussed; namely, whether some tribes represent a lower cultural stage when looked at from an evolutionary point of view.

Our previous discussion has shown that almost all attempts to characterize the mind of primitive man do not take into account racial affiliations, but only stages of culture, and the results of our efforts to determine characteristic racial differences have been of doubtful value. It appears, therefore, that modern anthropologists not only proceed on the assumption of the generic unity of the mind of man, but tacitly disregard quantitative differences which may very well occur. We may therefore base our further considerations on the theory of the similarity of mental functions in all races.

Observation has shown, however, that not only emotions, intellect, and will-power of man are alike everywhere, but that much more detailed similarities in thought and action occur among the most diverse peoples.

These similarities are apparently so detailed and far-reaching, that Bastian was led to speak of the appalling monotony of the fundamental ideas of mankind all over the globe.

Thus it has been found that the metaphysical notions of man may be reduced to a few types which are of universal distribution. The same is the case in regard to the forms of society, laws, and inventions.

Furthermore, the most intricate and apparently illogical ideas, and the most curious and complex customs, appear among a few tribes here and there in such a manner that the assumption of a common historical origin is excluded. When studying the culture of any one tribe, more or less close analogues of single traits of its culture may be found among a great diversity of peoples. Instances of such analogues have been collected to a vast extent by Tylor, Spencer, Frazer, Bastian, Andree, Post, and many others, so that it is not necessary to give here any detailed proof of this fact. A few examples will suffice. Among the more general ideas, I may mention the belief in a land of the souls of the deceased, located in the west, and reached by crossing a river, — known to all of us from Greek mythology, but well known also among the native tribes of America and Polynesia. Another example is the idea of a multiplicity of worlds, — one or more spanned over us, others stretching under us, the central one the home of man; the upper or lower, the home of the gods and happy souls; the other, the home of the unhappy, — an idea familiar to us from the positions of heaven and hell, but no less developed in India, Siberia, and arctic America. The idea of the ability of man to acquire protecting guardian spirits offers another example. Another domain of mental life furnishes equally striking instances. The universal knowledge of the art of producing fire by friction, the boiling of food, the knowledge of the drill, illustrate the universality of certain inventions. Still other phenomena of this class are furnished by certain elementary features of grammatical structure, like the use of expressions for the three persons of the pronoun, — namely, the speaker, the person addressed, and the person spoken of, — or the frequent distinction of singularity and plurality.

Special curious analogues that occur in regions far apart may be exemplified by such beliefs as the possibility of foretelling the future by the cracking of burnt bones (Andree), the occurrence of the Phaeton legend in Greece and northwest America (Boas), the bleeding of animals by the use of a small bow and arrow (Heger), the development of astrology in the Old World and the New, the similarity of basketry technique and design in Africa and America (Dixon), the invention of the blow-gun in America and Malaysia.

These examples will suggest the classes of phenomena to which I refer.   It follows from these observations that when we find analogues of single traits of culture among distinct peoples, the presumption is, not that there has been a common historical source, but that they have arisen independently; and the theory suggests itself that a common cause accounts for the constant recurrence of these phenomena among the most varied members of mankind, no matter to what race they may belong.

Further investigation shows that these customs are not quite evenly distributed, but that certain more or less intimate associations exist between the industrial development, social organization, and religious beliefs of the peoples of the world; so that, among people with simple industries, thoughts are found that differ somewhat from those of people who have advanced further in the development of material culture.   It has also been noticed that a relation exists between the ethnic life of a people and the geographical environment that favors or hinders their material development.

The common cause for this similarity of actions and beliefs of peoples and tribes widely separated, belonging to different races, and being on certain stages of cultural development, has been looked for in several ways.

Some investigators — like Ratzel, and in older times Karl Ritter and Guyot — have laid particular stress upon the influence of geographical environment upon the life of man, and emphasize those similarities which appear in similar types of environment.

Others believe that many of the customs, beliefs, and inventions common to people who live in regions far apart are an old heritage derived from the earliest times, when mankind was still confined to a small part of the earth's surface.

Still others have tried to isolate the most generalized forms of similar ethnic phenomena. Bastian, the most important representative of this group of investigators, has called these forms "elementary ideas," and has tried to show that they are unexplainable.

Psychologists finally have endeavored to explain the similarities by an analysis of mental processes.

It seems necessary to discuss these four methods of approach a little more fully.

It is not difficult to illustrate the important influence

of geographical environment upon forms of inventions. The variety of habitations used by tribes of different areas offer an example of its influence. The snow house of the Eskimo, the bark wigwam of the Indian, the cave dwelling of the tribes of the desert, may serve as illustrations of the way in which protection against exposure is attained, in accordance with the available materials. Other examples may be found in the forms of more special inventions : as in the complex bows of the Eskimo, which seem to be due to the lack of long elastic material for bow-staves; and in the devices for securing elasticity of the bow where elastic wood is difficult to obtain, or where greater strength of the bow is required ; and in the skin receptacles and baskets which often serve as substitutes for pottery among tribes without permanent habitation. We may also mention the dependence of the location of villages upon the food-supply, and of communication upon available trails or upon the facility of communication by water. Environmental influences appear in the territorial limits of certain tribes or peoples, as well as in the distribution and density of population. Even in the more complex forms of the mental life, the influence of environment may be found; as in nature myths explaining the activity of volcanoes or the presence of curious land forms, or in beliefs and customs relating to the local characterization of the seasons.

When, in our theories, we lay stress alone on observations which show that man is dependent upon geographical environment, and upon the assumption of a sameness or similarity of the mind in all races of mankind, we are necessarily led to the conclusion that the same environment will produce the same cultural results everywhere.

This is obviously not true, for the forms of culture of peoples living in the same kind of environment show often marked differences. I do not need to illustrate this by comparing the American settler with the North American Indian, or the successive races of people that have settled in England, and have developed from the Stone Age to the modern English. It may, however, be desirable to show that even among primitive tribes, geographical environment alone does not by any means determine the type of culture. Proof of this fact may be found in the mode of life of the hunting and fishing Eskimo and the reindeer-breeding Chukchee (Bogoras); the African pastoral Hottentot and the hunting Bushmen in their older, wider distribution (Schultze); the Negrito and the Malay of southeastern Asia (Martin).

A second and more important element to be considered

is the social status of each people, and it would seem that environment is important only in so far as it limits or favors the activities that belong to any particular group. It may even be shown that old customs, that may have been in harmony with a certain type of environment, tend to survive under new conditions, where they are of disadvantage rather than of advantage to the people.   An example of this kind, taken from our own civilization, is our failure to utilize unfamiliar kinds of food that may be found in newly settled countries.   Another example is presented by the reindeer-breeding Chukchee, who carry about in their nomadic life a tent of most complicated structure, which corresponds in its type to the older permanent house of the coast dwellers, and which contrasts in the most marked way with the simplicity and light weight of the Eskimo tent (Bogoras).   Even among the Eskimo, who have so marvellously well succeeded in adapting themselves to their geographical environment, we may recognize customs that prevent the fullest use of the opportunities offered by the country, an example of which is the law forbidding the promiscuous use of caribou-meat and of seal-meat (Boas).

Thus it would seem that environment has an important effect upon the customs and beliefs of man, but only in so far as it helps to determine the special forms of customs and beliefs. These are, however, based primarily on cultural conditions, which in themselves are due to historical causes.

At this point the students of anthropo-geography who attempt to explain the whole cultural development on the basis of geographical environmental conditions are wont to claim that these historical causes themselves are founded on older conditions, in which they have originated under the stress of environment. It seems to my mind that this claim is inadmissible as long as the investigation of every single cultural feature demonstrates that the influence of environment brings about a certain degree of adjustment between environment and social life, but that a complete explanation of the prevailing conditions, based on the action of environment alone, is never possible. We must remember, that, no matter how great an influence we may ascribe to environment, that influence can become active only by being exerted upon the mind ; so that the characteristics of the mind must enter into the resultant forms of social activity. It is just as little conceivable that mental life can be explained satisfactorily by environment alone, as that environment can be explained by the influence of the people upon nature, which, as we all know, has brought about changes of water-courses, the destruction of forests, and changes of fauna. In other words, it seems entirely arbitrary to disregard the part that psychical elements play in determining the forms of activities and beliefs which occur with great frequency all over the world.

The second theory that has been advanced to explain the sameness of a number of fundamental ideas and inventions is based on the assumption that they represent old cultural achievements belonging to a period previous to the general dispersion of the human race.

This theory is based on the universal distribution of certain cultural elements. Obviously it can apply only to features that occur the world over; for, if we should admit the loss of some of them in the course of historical development, the door would be open to the most fanciful conclusions. A few ethnological data seem to favor this theory, and make us inclined to believe that some of the universal traits of culture may go back to a very early time before that dispersion of mankind which is demanded on biological grounds. Most important among these is perhaps the occurrence of the dog as a domesticated animal in practically all parts of the world. It is true that in all probability native wild dogs constitute the principal ancestry of the dogs of the various continents; but nevertheless, it seems plausible that the living-together of man and dog developed in the earliest period of human history, before the races of northern Asia and America separated from those of southeastern Asia. The introduction of the dingo (the native dog) into Australia seems to be most easily explained when we assume that it accompanied man to that remote continent.

Other very simple activities may perhaps be derived from achievements of the earliest ancestors of man. The art of fire-making, of drilling, cutting, sawing, work in stone, belonged probably to this early age, and may have been the heritage on which each people built up its own individual type of culture (Weule). If archæological investigations should show that implements and other evidences of human achievement are found in a geological period during which mankind had not attained its present world-wide distribution, we should have to infer that these represent the early cultural possessions of man, which he carried with him all over the world. In this lies the great and fundamental importance of the eolithic finds that have been discussed so extensively during the last few years. Language is also a trait common to all mankind, and one that therefore may have its roots in earliest times.

The activities of the higher apes seem to favor the assumption that certain arts may have belonged to man before his dispersion.   Their habit of making nests, that is, habitations, the use of sticks and stones, point in this direction.

All this makes it plausible that certain cultural achievements date back to the origin of mankind.   The defenders of this theory, like Weule and Graebner, also believe that a sporadic occurrence of certain inventions like the boomerang, among races that are held to be akin in descent, may have originated before the differentiation and dispersion of these races.

In the case of many of the phenomena which may be explained from these points of view, it is quite impossible to give incontrovertible arguments which would prove that these customs are not due to parallel and independent development rather than to community of origin: the decision of this problem will be found largely in the results of prehistoric archæology on the one hand, and in those of animal psychology on the other.

The problem is made still more difficult by the dissemination of cultural elements from tribe to tribe, from people to people, and from continent to continent, which can be proved to have existed from the earliest times on.

As an instance of the rapidity with which cultural achievements are transmitted may be mentioned the modern
history of some cultivated plants.   Tobacco and cassava
were introduced into Africa after the discovery of America, and it took little time for these plants to spread
over the whole continent; so that at present they enter
so deeply into the whole culture of the negro, that nobody
would suspect their foreign origin (Hahn).   We find in
the same way that the use of the banana has pervaded
almost the whole of South America (Von den Steinen);
and the history of Indian-corn is another example of the
incredible rapidity with which a useful cultural acquisi-
tion may spread over the whole world.   It is mentioned
as known in Europe in 1539, and, according to Dr. Laufer,
had reached China by way of Tibet between 1540 and
1570.

It is easy to show that similar conditions prevailed in
earlier times.   Victor Hehn's investigations show the
gradual and continuous increase of the number of domesticated animals and cultivated plants, due to their im-
portation from Asia.   The same process was going on in
prehistoric times.   The gradual spread of the Asiatic
horse, which was first used as a draught animal, later on
for riding, the spread of cattle over Africa and Europe, the

development of European grains, may serve as illustrations. The area over which these additions to the stock of human culture were spread is very large. We see most of them travel westward until they reach the Atlantic coast, and eastward to the shores of the Pacific Ocean. They also penetrated the African Continent. It may be that the use of milk was disseminated in a similar way; for when the people of the world enter into our historic knowledge, we find milk used all over Europe, Africa, and the western part of Asia.

Perhaps the best proof of transmission is contained in the folk-lore of the tribes of the world. Nothing seems to travel as readily as fanciful tales. We know of certain complex tales, which cannot possibly have been invented twice, that are told by the Berbers in Morocco, by the Italians, the Russians, in the jungles of India, in the highlands of Tibet, on the tundras of Siberia, and on the prairies of North America; so that perhaps the only parts of the world not reached by them are South Africa, Australia, Polynesia, and South America. The examples of such transmission are quite numerous, and we begin to see that the early inter-relation of the races of man was almost world-wide.

It follows from this observation that the culture of any

given tribe, no matter how primitive it may be, can be fully explained only when we take into consideration its inner growth as well as its relation to the culture of its near and distant neighbors, and the effect that they may have exerted.

It may be well to indicate here that there seem to have been two enormously large areas of extended diffusion. Our brief remarks on the distribution of cultivated plants and domesticated animals prove the existence of inter-relations between Europe, Asia, and North Africa, from the Atlantic to the Pacific Ocean. Other cultural traits corroborate this conclusion. The gradual spread of bronze from Central Asia westward and eastward, all over Europe and over China, the area in which the wheel is used, where agriculture with plough and with the help of domesticated animals is practised, show the same type of distribution (Hahn). We may recognize the sameness of characteristic traits in this area also in other respects. Oath and ordeal are highly developed in Europe, Africa, and Asia excepting the northeastern part of Siberia, while in America they are hardly known (Laasch). Other common features of the cultural types of the Old World appear also most clearly by contrast with con-ditions in America. One of these features is the importance of formal judicial procedure in the Old World, and its almost entire absence among all the tribes of North and South America, who, in their general cultural development, might well be compared with the African negroes. In the domain of folk-lore I would mention the frequency of the riddle, the proverb, and the moralizing fable, which are so characteristic of an enormous part of the Old World, while they are lacking in northeastern Siberia and in America. In all these features, Europe, a large part of Africa, and Asia except in its extreme northeastern part, and its island connection east of the Malay Archipelago, form a unit.

In a similar manner we may trace certain very general traits over a large part of America. Most convincing among these is the use of Indian-corn all over that part of America in which agriculture is practised; but we might also mention the development of a peculiar type of ceremonialism and of decorative art. It would seem as though the middle parts of America had played a role similar to that of Central Asia in the Old World, in so far as many of the most characteristic traits of civilization may have had their home here before the higher type of Central American and South American civilizations were developed.

The third point of view is represented by Bastian, who recognizes the great importance of geographical environment in modifying the analogous ethnic phenomena, but does not ascribe to them creative power. To him the sameness of the forms of thought found in regions wide apart suggested the existence of certain definite types of thought, no matter in what surroundings man may live, and what may be his social and psychical relations. These fundamental forms of thought, "that develop with iron necessity wherever man lives," were called by him "elementary ideas." He denies that it is possible to discover the ultimate sources of inventions, ideas, customs, and beliefs, which are of universal occurrence. They may be indigenous, they may be imported, they may have arisen from a variety of sources, but they are there. The human mind is so formed that it invents them spontaneously, or accepts them whenever they are offered to it. Bastian's theory of the permanence of these forms of thought seems to me related to Dilthey's conception of the limitation of possible types of philosophy; and the similarity of lines of thought of these two men appears also clearly in Bastian's constant references to the theories of philosophers as compared to the views held by primitive man. The important phenomenon in

Bastian's mind was the fundamental sameness of forms of human thought in all forms of culture, no matter whether they were advanced or primitive.

In the views as propounded by him, a certain kind of mysticism may be recognized, in so far as the elementary ideas are to his mind intangible entities. No further thought can possibly unravel their origin, because we ourselves are compelled to think in the forms of these elementary ideas.

To a certain extent a clear enunciation of the elementary idea gives us the psychological reason for its existence. To exemplify: The fact that the land of shadows is so often placed in the west suggests its localization at the place where the sun and the stars vanish. The mere statement that primitive man considers the animals as gifted with all the qualities of man shows that the analogy between many of the qualities of animals and human qualities has led to the view that all the qualities of animals are human. In other cases the causes are not so self-evident; for example, in the instance of widespread customs of restrictions of marriage which have puzzled many investigators. The difficulty of this problem is proved by the multitude of hypotheses that have been invented to explain it in all its varied phases.

The problem of the origin of elementary ideas has, however, been discussed from a psychological point of view; and the elaborate attempt by Wundt to work out a theory of folk-psychology, as well as the studies of psychological sociologists, indicate lines of attack of the problem.   To illustrate this point, I may mention the general discussion of the function of association in the beliefs of primitive people, given by Wundt, or the study of suggestion and hypnotism in primitive life, made by Stoll. A more detailed discussion of this method of treatment of the common elementary ideas may be deferred until a later time (see Chapter VIII).

VII. THE EVOLUTIONARY VIEWPOINT

I HAVE pointed out before that some of the older authors, like Gobineau, Klemm, Carus, Nott and Gliddon, assume characteristic mental differences between the races of man; and these have been revived by the growth of modern nationalism, with its exaggerated self-admiration of the Teutonic race, its Pan-slavism, and similar symptoms developing in other parts of the world; but these views are not supported by the results of un-biassed research.

There remains, however, one point of view to be considered, which might furnish a basis for investigation. The variety of forms in which the fundamental ideas occur were early correlated with general impressions regarding the degrees of civilization, and attention was directed to the recurrence of similar forms the world over, which appear to present an increasing degree of complexity of culture. This led anthropologists to the conclusion that the types of human culture represent an evolutionary series; that the primitive tribes of our times represent an older stage of cultural development, through which the more advanced types passed in earlier periods. If this is true, and if, furthermore, it could be shown that the single tribes develop independently, we might well say that those races must be less favorably developed in which earlier types of culture are found with great frequency, later developments rarely. I have referred to this possibility at another place (p. 125). For this reason the theory of a uniform development of human civilization must be considered in our investigation of the relation between racial types and cultural progress. The investigations of Tylor and Bachofen, Morgan and Spencer, fixed the attention upon the data of anthropology as illustrating the gradual development and rise of civilization. The development of this side of anthropology was stimulated by the work of Darwin and his successors, and its fundamental ideas can be understood only as an application of the theory of biological evolution to mental phenomena. The conception that the manifestations of ethnic life represent a series, which from simple beginnings has progressed to the complex type of modern civilization, has been the underlying thought of this aspect of anthropological science.

The arguments in support of the theory that the

development of civilization has followed a similar course everywhere, and that among primitive tribes we may still recognize the stages through which our own civilization has passed, are largely based on the similarities of types of culture found in distinct races the world over, but also on the occurrence of peculiar customs in our own civilization, which can be understood only as survivals (Tylor) of older customs, that had a deeper significance at an earlier time, and which are still found in full vigor among primitive people.

It is necessary to point out at least a few of the aspects of this general problem, in order to make clear the significance of the evolutionary theory of human civilization.

The social organization of primitive tribes shows similar traits in many different parts of the world. Instead of counting descent in the way we do, many tribes consider the child as a member only of its mother's family, and count blood-relationship only in the maternal line, so that cousins on the mother's side are considered as near relatives, while cousins on the father's side are considered as only distantly related; other tribes have a strict paternal organization, so that the child belongs only to the father's family, not to the mother's; while still others follow the same principles as we adhere to, reckoning relationship in both directions.   Connected with these customs is the selection of the domicile of the newly married couple, who sometimes reside with the wife's tribe or family, sometimes with the man's tribe or family.   When the couple take up their residence with the social group to which the wife belongs, it is often found that the man is treated as a stranger until his first child is born.   These phenomena have been made the subject of thorough studies, and the observation has been made that apparently the customs of residence and of descent are closely associated (Tylor). As a result of these inquiries, the conclusion has been drawn that everywhere maternal institutions precede paternal institutions, and that the social organization of mankind was such that originally perhaps no distinct family organization existed ; that later on maternal institutions developed, which in turn were followed by paternal institutions, and again by the system of counting blood-relationship equally in maternal and paternal lines.

Similar results were obtained by the study of human inventions.   It has been noted before that apes and monkeys sometimes use stones for defence, and in a way the artificial shelters of animals indicate the beginnings of invention.   In this sense we may seek for the origin of implements and utensils among animals.   In the earliest times when human remains appear on the surface of the earth, we find man using simple stone implements which are formed by rough chipping, but the multiplicity of forms of implements increases gradually. Since many implements may have been made of perishable materials, we are not able to tell whether at a very early time the implements and utensils used were really confined to the few stone objects that may now be recovered; but certainly the implements were few, and, comparatively speaking, simple. From this time on, the uses of fire, and of tools for cutting and striking, for scraping and perforating, have increased in number and complexity, and a gradual development may be traced from the simple tools of primitive man to the complex machinery of our times. The inventive genius of all races and of unnumbered individuals has contributed to the state of industrial perfection in which we find ourselves. On the whole, inventions once made have been kept with great tenacity, and, owing to incessant additions, the available resources of mankind have constantly been increased and multiplied.

An excellent example of the general theory of evolution of civilization is found in the theory of evolution of agriculture and of the domestication of animals as outlined by Otis T. Mason, W J McGee, and Hahn. They point out how, in the earliest beginnings of social life, animals, plants, and man lived together in a definite surrounding, and how, owing to the conditions of life, certain plants multiplied to the exclusion of others, and how certain animals were suffered in the neighborhood of the human camp. Through this condition of mutual sufferance and promotion of mutual interests, if I may use this term, a closer association between plants, animals, and man developed, which ultimately led to the beginnings of agriculture and to the actual domestication of animals.

Researches on art have led to similar results. Investigators have endeavored to show, that, since the cave-dwellers of France drew the outlines of the reindeer and mammoth on bone and antler, man has tried to reproduce in pictographic design the animals of the region in which he lived. In the artistic productions of many people, designs have been found which are readily associated with pictographic presentations, which, however, have lost their realism of form, and have become more and more conventional; so that in many cases a purely decorative motive has been interpreted as developed from a realistic pictograph gradually breaking up under the stress of æsthetic motives. The islands of the Pacific Ocean,

New Guinea, South America, Central America, prehistoric Europe, have furnished examples for this line of development (see March, Haddon, Von den Steinen, Holmes), which therefore was recognized as one of the important tendencies of the evolution of human decorative art, which was described as beginning with realism, and as leading through symbolic conventionalism to purely æsthetic motives.

Religion has furnished another example of typical evolution in human thought. At an early time man began to think and ponder about the phenomena of nature. Everything appeared to him in an anthropomorphic form of thought; and thus the first primitive concepts regarding the world came into being, in which the stone, the mountain, the heavenly orbs, were viewed as animate anthropomorphic beings endowed with will-power, and willing to help man or threatening to endanger him. The observation of the activities of man's own body and of his mind led to the formulation of the idea of a soul independent of the body; and with increasing knowledge and with increasing philosophic thought, religion and science grew out of these simple beginnings.

The sameness of all these phenomena in different parts of the world has been considered as proof not only of the fundamental unity of the mind of all the races of man, but also of the truth of the theory of evolution of civilization ; and thus a grand structure has been reared, in which we see our present civilization as the necessary outcome of the activities of all the races of man that have risen in one grand procession, from the simplest beginnings of culture, through periods of barbarism, to the stage of civilization that they now occupy.   The march has not been equally rapid ; for some are still lagging behind, while others have forged forward, and occupy the first places in the general advance.

It seems desirable to understand more clearly what this theory of parallelism of cultural development implies.   It seems to mean that different groups of mankind started at a very early time from a general condition of lack of culture ; and, owing to the unity of the human mind and the consequent similar response to outer and inner stimuli, they have developed everywhere approximately along the same lines, making similar inventions and developing similar customs and beliefs. It also seems to involve a certain correlation between industrial development and social development, and therefore a definite sequence of inventions as well as of forms of organization and of belief.

In the absence of historical data in regard to the earliest history of primitive man the world over, we have only three sources of historical proof of this assumption,— the evidence contained in the earliest history of the civilized people of the Old World, survivals in modern civilization, and archæology. The last-named is the only method by means of which we can approach the problem in regard to people that have no history.

While it is certainly true that analogues can be found between the types of culture represented by primitive people and those conditions which prevailed among the ancestors of the present civilized peoples at the dawn of history, and that these analogues are supported by the evidence furnished by survivals, the evidence of archæology does not support the complete generalization. The theory of parallel development, if it is to have any significance, would require that among all branches of mankind the steps of invention should have followed, at least approximately, in the same order, and that no important gaps should be found. The facts, so far as known at the present time, are entirely contrary to this view. We find, for instance, large areas of the world inhabited by people well advanced in the arts of life, but who have never made the discovery of pottery, one of the essential steps in the advance of civilization. Pottery is not found in the extreme southern parts of Africa, in Australia, in northeastern Siberia,[1] in the whole northwestern part of North America, and in the extreme south of South America. According to what has been said before (p. 169), it would seem as if Old-World pottery covers about the same territory as the other characteristic traits referred to before, while in America its centre lies in the area of more advanced culture in the middle part of the continent. Thus it happens that the well-advanced tribes of Northwest America have no pottery, and its presence or absence seems to be due more to geographical location than to general cultural causes.

The same may be said in regard to the use of metals. The invention of metallurgy, which marks so important an advance of European civilization, does not appear associated with analogous levels of development in other parts of the world. Similar remarks may be made in regard to the development of agriculture and of the domestication of animals. People whom in a general way we ought to class as on the same level of culture may some possess the art of agriculture, others may have

---

[1] In a few localities in this district pottery is found, perhaps due to a late local introduction.

domesticated animals, while still others may rely upon the bounty of the sea or upon the natural vegetable products of their home.[1]   As soon as we begin to investigate the industrial achievements of different types belonging to different races, parallelism of industrial development does not seem to exist in any degree of detail.   Only one general trait of industrial development remains ; namely, the constant addition of new elements to the older stock of knowledge and an increasing refinement of methods and of results, setting aside periods of temporary regression.

Thus it does not seem to be certain that every people in an advanced stage of civilization must have passed through all the stages of development, which we may gather by an investigation of all the types of culture which occur all over the world.

A still more serious objection is based on another observation.   The validity of the general sameness of the evolution of mankind is based on the assumption that the same cultural features must always have developed from the same causes, and that all variations are only minor details of the grand uniform type of evolution.   In other words, its logical basis is the assumption that the same

[1] The cultural conditions of Melanesia Northwest America, and of some of the nomadic tribes of Africa, might thus be compared.

ethnical phenomena are always due to the same causes. Thus the inference in regard to the sequence of maternal and paternal institutions, to which I referred before, is based on the generalization that because in a few cases paternal families have developed from maternal ones, therefore all paternal families have developed in the same way. If we do not make the assumption that the same phenomena have everywhere developed in the same way, then we may just as well conclude that paternal families have in some cases arisen from maternal institutions, in other cases in other ways.

In the same way it is inferred that because many conceptions of the future life have evidently developed from dreams and hallucinations, all notions of this character have had the same origin. This is true only if it can be shown that no other causes could possibly lead to the same ideas.

To give another example. It has been claimed that among the Indians of Arizona, pottery developed from basketry, and it has been inferred that all pottery must therefore be later in the cultural development of mankind than basketry. Evidently this conclusion cannot be defended, for pottery may develop in other ways.

As a matter of fact, quite a number of cases can be given

in which convergent evolution, beginning from distinct beginnings, has led to the same results. I have referred before to the instance of primitive art, and have mentioned the theory that geometrical form develops from realistic representations, which lead through symbolic conventionalism to purely æsthetic motives. We may remark here that a great diversity of objects might in this way have given rise to the same decorative motives, so that the survival of the same decorative motive would not lead back to the same realistic origin ; but more important than this, we may point out that geometrical motives of the same type have developed from the tendency of the artist to play with his technique as the virtuoso plays on his instrument ; that the expert basket-weaver, by varying the arrangement of her weave, was led to the development of geometrical designs of the same form as those that were developed in other places from realistic representations. We may even go a step farther, and recognize that geometrical forms developed from the technique suggested animal forms, which later on were modified so as to assume realistic forms ; so that in the case of decorative art the same forms may just as well stand at the beginning of a series of development as at the end (Von den Steinen).

Another example may not be amiss. The use of masks is found among a great number of peoples. The origin of the custom is by no means clear in all cases, but a few typical forms of their use may easily be distinguished. They are intended to deceive spirits as to the identity of the wearer, and may thus protect him against attack; or the mask may represent a spirit which is personified by the wearer, who in this way frightens away supernatural enemies. Still other masks are commemorative, the wearer personifying a deceased friend. Masks are also used in theatrical performances illustrating mythological incidents (Andree). While it is not at all necessary to assume that these explanations given by the wearer of masks represent the actual historical development of the custom, the explanations themselves suggest the improbability of a single origin of the custom.

I will give another example. Primitive tribes are very often divided into a definite number of subdivisions. There is little doubt that this form of social organization has arisen independently over and over again. The conclusion is justified that the psychical conditions of man favor the existence of such an organization of society, but it does not follow that it has developed everywhere in the same manner. Dr. Washington Matthews has shown that the groups of the Navaho have arisen by the association of independent elements. Captain Bourke has pointed out that similar occurrences have given rise to the Apache groups, and Dr. Fewkes has reached the same conclusion in regard to some of the Pueblo tribes. On the other hand, we have proof that such groups may originate by division. Such events have taken place among the Indians of the North Pacific coast (Boas). Other divisions of tribes seem to have had an entirely different origin; as, for instance, the frequent twofold exogamic division of tribes, which may, perhaps, be adequately explained by the application of the laws of exogamy in a small community. Thus it would seem that a variety of causes has led to results which appear identical to all intents and purposes.

The principal obstacle in the way of progress on these lines seems to my mind to be founded on the lack of comparability of the data with which we are dealing. Attention has been directed essentially to the similarity of ethnic phenomena, while the individual variations were disregarded. As soon as we turn our attention in this direction, we notice that the sameness of ethnic phenomena is more superficial than complete, more apparent than real. The unexpected similarities have attracted our attention to such an extent that we have disregarded differences; while in the study of the physical traits of distinct social groups, the reverse mental attitude manifests itself. The similarity of the main features of the human form being self-evident, our attention is directed to the minute differences of structure.

Instances of such lack of comparability can easily be given. When we speak of the idea of life after death as one of the ideas which develop in human society as a psychological necessity, we are dealing with a most complex group of data. One people believes that the soul continues to exist in the form that the person had at the time of death, without any possibility of change; another one believes that the soul will be reborn in a child of the same family; a third one believes that the souls will enter the bodies of animals; and still others believe that the shadows continue our human pursuits, waiting to be led back to our world in a distant future. The emotional and rationalistic elements which enter into these various concepts are entirely distinct; and we can readily perceive how the various forms of the idea of a future life may have come into existence by psychological processes that are not at all comparable. If I may be allowed to speculate on this question, I might imagine that in one case the similarities between children and their deceased relatives, in other cases the memory of the deceased as he lived during the last days of his life, in still other cases the longing for the beloved child or parent, and again the fear of death, — may all have contributed to the development of the idea of life after death, the one here, the other there.

Another instance will corroborate this point of view. One of the striking forms of social organization which occurs in many regions wide apart is what we call "totemism," — a form of society in which certain social groups consider themselves as related in a supernatural way to a certain species of animals or to a certain class of objects. I believe this is the generally accepted definition of "totemism;" but I am convinced that in this form the phenomenon is not a single psychological problem, but embraces the most diverse psychological elements. In some cases the people believe themselves to be descendants of the animal whose protection they enjoy. In other cases an animal or some other object may have appeared to an ancestor of the social group, and may have promised to become his protector, and the friendship between the animal and the ancestor was then transmitted to his descendants. In still other cases a certain social group in a tribe may have the power of securing by magical means and with great ease a certain kind of animal or of increasing its numbers, and the supernatural relation may be established in this way. It will be recognized that here again the anthropological phenomena which are in outward appearances alike are, psychologically speaking, entirely distinct, and that consequently psychological laws covering all of them cannot be deduced from them (Goldenweiser).

Another example may not be amiss. In a general review of moral standards we observe that with increasing civilization a gradual change in the valuation of actions takes place. Among primitive man, human life has little value, and is sacrificed on the slightest provocation. The social group among whose members any altruistic obligations are binding is exceedingly small; and outside of the group any action that may result in personal gain is not only permitted, but even approved ; and from this starting-point we find an ever-increasing valuation of human life and an extension of the size of the group among whose members altruistic obligations are binding. The modern relations of nations show that this evolution has not yet reached its final stage. It might seem, therefore, that a study of the social conscience in relation to crimes like murder might be of psychological value, and lead to important results, clearing up the origin of ethical values; but I think here the same objections may be raised as before; namely, the lack of comparable motives. The person who slays an enemy in revenge for wrongs done, a youth who kills his father before he gets decrepit in order to enable him to continue a vigorous life in the world to come, a father who kills his child as a sacrifice for the welfare of his people, act from such entirely different motives, that psychologically a comparison of their activities does not seem permissible. It would seem much more proper to compare the murder of an enemy in revenge with destruction of his property for the same purpose, or to compare the sacrifice of a child on behalf of the tribe with any other action performed on account of strong altruistic motives, than to base our comparison on the common concept of murder (Westermarck).

These few data may suffice to show that the same ethnic phenomenon may develop from different sources; and we may infer that the simpler the observed fact, the more likely it is that it may have developed from one source here, from another there.

When we base our study on these observations, it appears that serious objections may be made against the assumption of the occurrence of a general sequence of cultural stages among all the races of man ; that rather we recognize a peculiar tendency of diverse customs and beliefs to converge towards similar forms.   In order to interpret correctly these similarities in form, it is necessary to investigate their historical development ; and only when the historical development in different areas is the same, will it be admissible to consider the phenomena in question as equivalent.   From this point of view the facts of cultural contact assume a new importance (see p. 166).

An important theoretical consideration has also shaken our faith in the correctness of the evolutionary theory as a whole.   It is one of the essential traits of this theory that, in general, civilization has developed from simple forms to complex forms, and that extended fields of human culture have developed under more or less rationalistic impulses.   Of late years we are beginning to recognize that human culture does not always develop from the simple to the complex, but that in many aspects two tendencies intercross, — one from the complex to the simple, the other from the simple to the complex.   It is obvious that the history of industrial development is almost throughout that of increasing complexity.   On the other hand, human activities that do not depend upon reasoning do not show a similar type of evolution.

It is perhaps easiest to make this clear by the example of language, which in many respects is one of the most important evidences of the history of human development. Primitive languages are, on the whole, complex. Minute differences in point of view are given expression by means of grammatical forms; and the grammatical categories of Latin, and still more so those of modern English, seem crude when compared to the complexity of psychological or logical forms which primitive languages recognize, but which in our speech are disregarded entirely. On the whole, the development of languages seems to be such, that the nicer distinctions are eliminated, and that it begins with complex and ends with simpler forms, although it must be acknowledged that opposite tendencies are not by any means absent (Boas).

Similar observations may be made on the art of primitive man. In music as well as in decorative design we find a complexity of rhythmic structure which is unequalled in the popular art of our day. In music, particularly, this complexity is so great, that the art of a skilled virtuoso is taxed in the attempt to imitate it (Stumpf). If once it is recognized that simplicity is not always a proof of antiquity, it will readily be seen that the theory of the evolution of civilization rests to a certain extent on a logical error.   The classification of the data of anthropology in accordance with their simplicity has been reinterpreted as an historical sequence, without an adequate attempt to prove that the simpler antedates the more complex.

We are thus led to the conclusion that the assumption of a uniform development of culture among all the different races of man and among all tribal units is true in a limited sense only.   We may recognize a certain modification of mental activities with modifications of form of culture ; but the assumption that the same forms must necessarily develop in every independent social unit can hardly be maintained.   Thus the question with which we began our consideration — namely, whether the representatives of different races can be proved to have developed each independently, in such a way that the representatives of some races stand on low levels of culture, while others stand on high levels of culture — may be answered in the negative.   If we should make the attempt to arrange the different types of man in accordance with their industrial advancement, we should find representatives of the most diverse races — such as the Bushman of

South Africa, the Veddah of Ceylon, the Australian, and the Indian of Terra del Fuego — on the same lowest level. We should also find representatives of different races on more advanced levels, like the negroes of Central Africa, the Indians of the Southwestern pueblos, and the Polynesians; and in our present period we may find representatives of the most diverse races taking part in the highest types of civilization. Thus it will be seen that there is no close relation between race and culture.

VIII. SOME TRAITS OF PRIMITIVE CULTURE

IT now remains to formulate more clearly the difference between the forms of thought of primitive man and those of civilized man, regardless of their racial descent.

Even a superficial observation demonstrates that groups of man belonging to distinct social strata do not behave in the same manner. The Russian peasant does not re-act to his sense-experiences in the same way as does the native Australian; and entirely different from theirs are the re-actions of the educated Chinaman and of the educated American. In all these cases the form of re-action may depend to a slight extent upon hereditary individual and racial ability, but it will to a much greater extent be determined by the habitual re-actions of the society to which the individual in question belongs.

It seems necessary, therefore, as a last step in our discussion, to define and explain the mental re-actions which distinguish primitive man and civilized man of all races.

We must confine this discussion to a very few examples of fundamental psychological facts.

One of the most striking features in the thoughts of primitive people is the peculiar manner in which concepts that appear to us alike and related are separated and re-arranged. According to our views, the constituting elements of the heavens and of the weather are all inanimate objects; but to the mind of primitive man they appear to belong to the organic world. The dividing-line between man and animal is not sharply drawn. What seem to us conditions of an object — like health and sickness — are considered by him as independent realities. In short, the whole classification of experience among mankind living in different forms of society follows entirely distinct lines.

I have illustrated the necessity of classification in a previous chapter, when speaking of the relation of language and cultural development (p. 143). Incidentally I have also pointed out that the principles of classification which are found in different languages do not by any means agree.

The behavior of primitive man makes it perfectly clear that all these linguistic classes have never risen into consciousness, and that consequently their origin must be sought, not in rational, but in entirely unconscious, processes of the mind. They must be due to a grouping of sense-impressions and of concepts which is not in any sense of the term voluntary, but which develops from entirely different psychological causes. It is a characteristic of linguistic classifications that they never rise into consciousness; while other classifications, although the same unconscious origin prevails, often do rise into consciousness. It seems very plausible, for instance, that the fundamental religious notions, like the idea of will-power immanent in inanimate objects, or the anthropomorphic character of animals, are in their origin just as little conscious as the fundamental ideas of language. While, however, the use of language is so automatic that the opportunity never arises for the fundamental notions to emerge into consciousness, this happens very frequently in all phenomena relating to religion.

These observations may be applied equally well to other groups of concepts.

The primary object of these researches is the determination of the fundamental categories under which phenomena are classified by man in various stages of culture. Differences of this kind appear very clearly in the domain of certain simple sense-perceptions. For instance, it has been observed that colors are classified according to their similarities in quite distinct groups, without any accompanying difference in the ability to differentiate shades of color. What we call green and blue are often combined under some such term as "gall-like color"; or yellow and green are combined into one concept, which may be named "young-leaves color." The importance of the fact that in thought and in speech these color-names convey the impression of quite different groups of sensations can hardly be overrated.

Another group of categories that offer a field of fruitful investigation are those of object and attribute. The concepts of primitive man make it quite clear that the classes of ideas which we consider as attributes are often considered as independent objects. The best-known case of this kind, one to which I have referred incidentally before, is that of sickness. While we consider sickness as a condition of an organism, it is believed by primitive man, and even by many members of our own society, to be an object which may enter the body, and which may be removed. This is exemplified by the numerous cases in which a disease is extracted from the body by sucking or by other processes, in the belief that it may be thrown into people, or that it may be enclosed in wood in order to prevent its return. Other qualities are treated in the same way. Thus the conditions of hunger, exhaustion, and similar bodily feelings, are considered by certain primitive tribes as independent objects which affect the body. Even life is believed to be a material object that may become separated from the body. The luminosity of the sun is considered as an object that the Sun himself may put on or lay aside.

I have indicated before that the concept of anthropomorphism seems to be one of the important categories underlying primitive thought. It would seem that the power of motion of the self, and the power of motion of an object, have led to the inclusion of man and movable objects in the same category, with the consequent imputation of human qualities to the moving objective world.

While in many cases we can see with a fair degree of clearness the fundamental concepts underlying these categories, in other cases these are not by any means clear. Thus the concept of incest groups — those groups in which intermarriage is strictly forbidden — is omnipresent; but no satisfactory explanation has so far been given for the tendency to combine certain degrees of blood-relationship under this viewpoint.

Another fundamental difference between the mental life of primitive man and that of civilized man lies in the fact that we have succeeded in developing, by the application of conscious reasoning, better systems from these crude, unconscious classifications of the sum total of our knowledge, while primitive man has not done so. ⌐The first impression gained from a study of the beliefs of primitive man is, that while the perceptions of his senses are excellent, his power of logical interpretation of perceptions seems to be deficient. I think it can be shown that the reason for this fact is not founded on any fundamental peculiarity of the mind of primitive man, but lies, rather, in the character of the traditional ideas by means of which each new perception is interpreted ; in other words, in the character of the traditional ideas with which each new perception associates itself. In our own community a mass of observations and of thoughts is transmitted to the child. These thoughts are the result of careful observation and speculation of our present and of past generations ; but they are transmitted to most individuals as traditional matter, much the same as folk-lore. The child associates new perceptions with this whole mass of traditional material, and interprets his observations by its means. ⌐I believe it is a mistake to assume that the interpretation made by each civilized individual is a complete logical process. We associate a phenomenon with a number of known facts, the interpretations of which are assumed as known, and we are satisfied with the reduction of a new fact to these previously known facts.   For instance, if the average individual hears of the explosion of a previously unknown chemical, he is satisfied to reason that certain materials are known to have the property of exploding under proper conditions, and that consequently the unknown substance has the same quality.   On the whole, I do not think that we should try to argue still further, and really try to give a full explanation of the causes of the explosion.

The difference in the mode of thought of primitive man and that of civilized man seems to consist largely in the difference of character of the traditional material with which the new perception associates itself.   The instruction given to the child of primitive man is not based on centuries of experimentation, but consists of the crude experience of generations.   When a new experience enters the mind of primitive man, the same process which we observe among civilized man brings about an entirely different series of associations, and therefore results in a different type of explanation.   A sudden explosion will associate itself in his mind, perhaps, with tales which he has heard in regard to the mythical history of the world, and consequently will be accompanied by superstitious fear. When we recognize that neither among civilized men nor among primitive men the average individual carries to completion the attempt at causal explanation of phenomena, but carries it only so far as to amalgamate it with other previously known facts, we recognize that the result of the whole process depends entirely upon the character of the traditional material. Herein lies the immense importance of folk-lore in determining the mode of thought. Herein lies particularly the enormous influence of current philosophic opinion upon the masses of the people, and herein lies the influence of the dominant scientific theory upon the character of scientific work.

It would be vain to try to understand the development of modern science without an intelligent understanding of modern philosophy; it would be vain to try to understand the history of mediæval science without a knowledge of mediæval theology; and so it is vain to try to understand primitive science without an intelligent knowledge of primitive mythology. "Mythology," "theology," and "philosophy" are different terms for the same influences which shape the current of human thought, and which determine the character of the attempts of man to explain the phenomena of nature. To primitive man, — who has been taught to consider the heavenly orbs as animate beings; who sees in every animal a being more powerful than man; to whom the mountains, trees, and stones are endowed with life, — explanations of phenomena will suggest themselves entirely different from those to which we are accustomed, since we base our conclusions upon the existence of matter and force as bringing about the observed results.   If we should not consider it possible to explain the whole range of phenomena as the result of matter and force alone, all our explanations of natural phenomena would take a different aspect.

In scientific inquiries we should always be clear in our own minds of the fact that we always embody a number of hypotheses and theories in our explanations, and that we do not carry the analysis of any given phenomenon to completion.   In fact, if we were to do so, progress would hardly be possible, because every phenomenon would require an endless amount of time for thorough treatment.   We are only too apt, however, to forget entirely the general, and for most of us purely traditional, theoretical basis which is the foundation of our reasoning, and to assume that the result of our reasoning is absolute truth.   In this we commit the same error that is committed, and has been committed, by all the less civilized peoples. They are more easily satisfied than we are at the present time; but they also assume as true the traditional element which enters into their explanations, and therefore accept as absolute truth the conclusions based on it. It is evident that the fewer the number of traditional elements that enter into our reasoning, and the clearer we endeavor to be in regard to the hypothetical part of our reasoning, the more logical will be our conclusions. There is an undoubted tendency in the advance of civilization to eliminate traditional elements, and to gain a clearer and clearer insight into the hypothetical basis of our reasoning. It is therefore not surprising, that, with the advance of civilization, reasoning becomes more and more logical, not because each individual carries out his thought in a more logical manner, but because the traditional material which is handed down to each individual has been thought out and worked out more thoroughly and more carefully. While in primitive civilization the traditional material is doubted and examined by only a very few individuals, the number of thinkers who try to free themselves from the fetters of tradition increases as civilization advances.

An example illustrating this progress and at the same

time the slowness of this progress is found in the relations between individuals belonging to different tribes.   There are a number of primitive hordes to whom every stranger not a member of the horde is an enemy, and where it is right to damage the enemy to the best of one's power and ability, and if possible to kill him.   This custom is founded largely on the idea of the solidarity of the horde, and of the feeling that it is the duty of every member of the horde to destroy all possible enemies.   Therefore every person not a member of the horde must be considered as belonging to a class entirely distinct from the members of the horde, and is treated accordingly.   We can trace the gradual broadening of the feeling of fellowship during the advance of civilization.   The feeling of fellowship in the horde expands to the feeling of unity of the tribe, to a recognition of bonds established by a neighborhood of habitat, and further on to the feeling of fellowship among members of nations.   This seems to be the limit of the ethical concept of fellowship of man which we have reached at the present time.   When we analyze the strong feeling of nationality which is so potent at the present time, we recognize that it consists largely in the idea of the pre-eminence of that community whose member we happen to be, — in the pre-eminent value of its language, of its customs, and of its traditions, and in the belief that it is right to preserve its peculiarities and to impose them upon the rest of the world. The feeling of nationality as here expressed, and the feeling of solidarity of the horde, are of the same order, although modified by the gradual expansion of the idea of fellowship; but the ethical point of view which makes it justifiable at the present time to increase the well-being of one nation at the cost of another, the tendency to value one's own civilization as higher than that of the whole rest of mankind, are the same as those which prompt the actions of primitive man, who considers every stranger as an enemy, and who is not satisfied until the enemy is killed. It is somewhat difficult for us to recognize that the value which we attribute to our own civilization is due to the fact that we participate in this civilization, and that it has been controlling all our actions since the time of our birth; but it is certainly conceivable that there may be other civilizations, based perhaps on different traditions and on a different equilibrium of emotion and reason, which are of no less value than ours, although it may be impossible for us to appreciate their values without having grown up under their influence. The general theory of valuation of human activities, as developed by anthro-

pological research, teaches us a higher tolerance than the
one which we now profess.

After we have thus seen that a large number of traditional elements enter into the reasoning of primitive man
and of civilized man as well, we are better prepared to
understand some of the more special typical differences in
the thought of primitive man and of civilized man.

A trait of primitive life that early attracted the attention of investigators is the occurrence of close associations
between mental activities that appear to us as entirely
disparate.   In primitive life, religion and science ; music,
poetry, and dance ; myth and history ; fashion and
ethics, — appear inextricably interwoven.   We may express this general observation also by saying that primitive man views each action not only as adapted to its
main object, each thought related to its main end, as we
should perceive them, but that he associates them with
other ideas, often of a religious or at least of a symbolic
nature.   Thus he gives them a higher significance than
they seem to us to deserve.   Every taboo is an example
of such associations of apparently trifling actions with
ideas that are so sacred that a deviation from the customary mode of performance creates the strongest emotions of abhorrence.   The interpretation of ornaments as

charms, the symbolism of decorative art, are other examples of association of ideas that, on the whole, are foreign to our mode of thought.

In order to make clear the point of view from which these phenomena seem to fall into an orderly array, we will investigate whether all vestiges of similar forms of thought have disappeared from our civilization. In our intense life, which is devoted to activities requiring the full application of our reasoning-powers and a repression of the emotional life, we have become accustomed to a cold, matter-of-fact view of our actions, of the incentives that lead to them, and of their consequences. It is not necessary, however, to go far afield to find a state of mind which is open to other aspects of life. If those among us who move in the midst of the current of our quickly pulsing life do not look beyond their rational motives and aims, others who stand by in quiet contemplation recognize in it the reflection of an ideal world that they have built up in their own consciousness. To the artist the outer world is a symbol of the beauty that he feels; to the fervent religious mind it is a symbol of the transcendental truth which gives form to his thought. Instrumental music that one enjoys as a work of purely musical art calls forth in the mind of another a group of definite con-

cepts that are connected with the musical themes and
their treatment only by the similarity of the emotional
states they evoke.   In fact, the different manner in which
individuals re-act to the same stimulus, and the variety
of associations elicited by the same sense-impression in
different individuals, are so self-evident that they hardly
call for special remarks.

Most important for the purpose of our investigation is
the fact that there are certain stimuli to which all of us
who live in the same society re-act in the same way without being able to express the reasons for our actions.   A
good example of what I refer to are breaches of social
etiquette.   A mode of behavior that does not conform
to the customary manners, but differs from them in a
striking way, creates, on the whole, unpleasant emotions;
and it requires a determined effort on our part to make
it clear to ourselves that such behavior does not conflict
with moral standards.   Among those who are not
trained in courageous and rigid thought, the confusion
between traditional etiquette — so-called good manners
— and moral conduct is habitual.   In certain lines of
conduct the association between traditional etiquette and
ethical feeling is so close, that even a vigorous thinker
can hardly emancipate himself from it.   This is true, for

instance, of acts that may be considered breaches of modesty. The most cursory review of the history of costume shows that what was considered modest at one time has been immodest at other times. The custom of habitually covering parts of the body has at all times led to the strong feeling that exposure of such parts is immodest. This feeling of propriety is so erratic, that a costume that is appropriate on one occasion may be considered opprobrious on other occasions; as, for instance, a low-cut evening dress in a street-car during business hours. What kind of exposure is felt as immodest depends always upon fashion. It is quite evident that fashion is not dictated by modesty, but that the historical development of costume is determined by a variety of causes. Nevertheless fashions are typically associated with the feeling of modesty, so that an unwonted exposure excites the unpleasant feelings of impropriety. There is no conscious reasoning why the one form is proper, the other improper; but the feeling is aroused directly by the contrast with the customary. Every one will feel instinctively the strong resistance that he would have to overcome, even in a different society, if he were required to perform an action that we are accustomed to consider as immodest, and the feelings that would be excited in his mind if he were thrown into a society in which the standards of modesty differed from our own.

Even setting aside the strong emotions of modesty, we find a variety of reasons which make certain styles of dress appear improper. To appear in the fashion of our forefathers of two centuries ago would be entirely out of the question, and would expose one to ridicule. To see a man wear a hat in company indoors nettles us: it is considered rude. To wear a hat in church or at a funeral would cause more vigorous resentment, on account of the greater emotional value of the feelings concerned. A certain tilt of the hat, although it may be very comfortable to the wearer, would stamp him at once as an uneducated brute. Other novelties in costume may hurt our æsthetic feelings, no matter how bad the taste of the prevailing fashions may be.

Another example will make clear what I mean. When we consider our table manners, it will readily be recognized that most of them are purely traditional, and cannot be given any adequate explanation. To smack one's lips is considered bad style, and may excite feelings of disgust; while among the Indians it would be considered bad taste not to smack one's lips when invited to dinner, because it would suggest that the guest does not enjoy his meal. Both for the Indian and for ourselves the constant performance of these actions which constitute good table manners make it practically impossible to act otherwise. An attempt to act differently would not only be difficult on account of the lack of adjustment of muscular motions, but also on account of the strong emotional resistance that we should have to overcome. The emotional displeasure is also released when we see others act contrary to custom. To eat with people having table manners different from our own excites feelings of displeasure which may rise to such an intensity as to cause qualmishness. Here, also, explanations are often given which are probably based solely on attempts to explain the existing manners, but which do not represent their historical development. We often hear that it is improper to eat with a knife because it might cut the mouth; but I doubt very much if this consideration has anything to do with the development of the custom, for the older type of sharp steel forks might as easily hurt the mouth as the blade of the knife.

It may be well to exemplify the characteristics of our opposition to unwonted actions by a few additional examples, which will help to clear up the mental processes that lead us to formulate the reasons for our conservatism.

One of the cases in which the development of such alleged reasons for behavior is best traced is that of the taboo. Although we ourselves have hardly any definite taboos, to an outsider our failure to use certain animals for food might easily appear from this point of view. Supposing an individual accustomed to eating dogs should inquire among us for the reason why we do not eat dogs, we could only reply that it is not customary; and he would be justified in saying that dogs are tabooed among us, just as much as we are justified in speaking of taboos among primitive people. If we were hard pressed for reasons, we should probably base our aversion to eating dogs or horses on the seeming impropriety of eating animals that live with us as our friends. On the other hand, we are not accustomed to eat caterpillars, and we should probably decline to eat them from feelings of disgust. Cannibalism is so much abhorred, that we find it difficult to convince ourselves that it belongs to the same class of aversions as those mentioned before. The fundamental concept of the sacredness of human life, and the fact that most animals will not eat others of the same species, set off cannibalism as a custom by itself, considered as one of the most horrible aberrations of human nature. In these three groups of aversions, disgust is probably the first feeling present in our minds, by which we re-act against the suggestion of partaking of these kinds of food. We account for our disgust by a variety of reasons, according to the groups of ideas with which the suggested act is associated in our minds. In the first case there is no special association, and we are satisfied with the simple statement of disgust. In the second case the most important reason seems to be an emotional one, although we may feel inclined, when questioned regarding the reasons of our dislike, to bring forward also habits of the animals in question that seem to justify our aversion. In the third case the immorality of cannibalism would stand forth as the one sufficient reason.

Other examples are the numerous customs that had originally a religious or semi-religious aspect, and which are continued and explained by more or less certain utilitarian theories. Such are the whole group of customs relating to marriages in the incest group. While the extent of the incest group has undergone material changes, the abhorrence of marriages inside the existing group is the same as ever; but instead of religious laws, ethical considerations, often explained by utilitarian concepts, are given as the reason for our feelings. People affected with loathsome diseases were once shunned because they were believed to be stricken by God, while at present the same avoidance is due to the fear of contagion. The disuse into which profanity has fallen in English was first due to religious re-action, but has come to be simply a question of good manners.

For another example we need go back only a short period in history. It is not so many years ago that dissension from accepted religious tenets was believed to be a crime. The intolerance of diverging religious views and the energy of persecution for heresy can be understood only when we recognize the violent feelings of outraged ethical principles that were aroused by this deviation from the customary line of thought. There was no question as to the logical validity of the new idea. The mind was directly agitated by the opposition to an habitual form of thought which was so deeply rooted in each individual that it had come to be an integral part of his mental life.

It is important to note that in all the cases mentioned the rationalistic explanation of the opposition to a change is based on that group of concepts with which the excited emotions are intimately connected. In the case of costume, reasons are adduced why the new style is improper; in the case of heresy, proof is given that the new doctrine is an attack against eternal truth; and so with all the others.

I think, however, that a close introspective analysis shows these reasons to be only attempts to interpret our feelings of displeasure; that our opposition is not by any means dictated by conscious reasoning, but primarily by the emotional effect of the new idea which creates a dissonance with the habitual.

In all these cases the custom is obeyed so often and so regularly that the habitual act becomes automatic; that is to say, its performance is ordinarily not combined with any degree of consciousness. Consequently the emotional value of these actions is also very slight. It is remarkable, however, that the more automatic an action, the more difficult it is to perform the opposite action, that it requires a very strong effort to do so, and that ordinarily the opposite action is accompanied by strong feelings of displeasure. It may also be observed that to see the unusual action performed by another person excites the strongest attention, and causes feelings of displeasure. Thus it happens that when an infraction of the customary occurs, all the groups of ideas with which the action is associated are brought into consciousness. A dish of dog's meat would bring up all the ideas of companionship; a cannibal feast, all the social principles that have become our second nature. The more automatic any series of activities or a certain form of thought has become, the greater is the conscious effort required for breaking away from the old habit of acting and thinking, and the greater also the displeasure, or at least the surprise, produced by an innovation. The antagonism against it is a reflex action accompanied by emotions not due to conscious speculation. When we become conscious of this emotional re-action, we endeavor to interpret it by a process of reasoning. This reason must necessarily be based on the ideas which rise into consciousness as soon as a break in the established custom occurs; in other words, our rationalistic explanation will depend upon the character of the associated ideas.

It is therefore of great importance to know whence the associated ideas are derived, particularly in how far we may assume that these associations are stable. It is not quite easy to give definite examples of changes of such associations in our civilization, because, on the whole, the rationalistic tendencies of our times have eliminated many of the lines of association, even where the emotional effect remains; so that the change, on the whole, is one from existing associations to loss of associations.

We may sum up these observations by saying, that, while each habit is the result of historical causes, it may in course of time associate itself with different ideas. As soon as we become conscious of an association between a habit and a certain group of ideas, we are led to explain the habit by its present associations, which probably differ from the associations prevailing at the time when the habit was established.

We will now turn to a consideration of analogous phenomena in primitive life. Here the dislike of that which deviates from the custom of the land is even more strongly marked than in our civilization. If it is not the custom to sleep in a house with feet turned towards the fire, a violation of this custom is dreaded and avoided. If in a certain society members of the same clan do not intermarry, the most deep-seated abhorrence against such unions will arise. It is not necessary to multiply examples, for it is a well-known fact that the more primitive a people, the more it is bound by customs regulating the conduct of daily life in all its details. I think we are justified in concluding from our own experience, that as among ourselves, so among primitive tribes, the resistance to a deviation from firmly established customs is due to an emotional re-action, not to conscious reasoning. This does not preclude the possibility that the first special act, which became in course of time customary, may have been due to a conscious mental process; but it seems to me likely that many customs came into being without any conscious activity. Their development must have been of the same kind as that of the categories which are reflected in the morphology of languages, and which can never have been known to the speakers of these languages. For instance, if we accept Cunow's theory of the origin of Australian social systems,[1] we may very well say that

[1] Some Australian tribes are divided into four exogamic groups. The laws of exogamy demand that a member of the first group must marry a member of the second group, and a member of the third group one of the fourth group. Cunow explains these customs by showing that when custom provides that a man in a tribe that is divided into two exogamic units, and in which only members of the same generation are allowed to intermarry, conditions like those found in Australia will naturally develop, if each group has a name, and one set of names are used for the first, third, fifth, generations, and another set of names for the second, fourth, sixth, generations, etc. If we should designate the two tribal divisions by the letters A and B, the generations by 1 and 2, the names of the four divisions would be A1, A2, B1, B2; and in marriages in which is placed first the sex that determines the group to which the offspring belongs, we find that —

A1 must marry B1, and his children are A2
B1 " " A1, " " " " B2
A2 " " B2, " " " " A1
B2 " " A2, " " " " B1

originally each generation kept by themselves, and therefore marriages between members of two succeeding generations were impossible, because only marriageable men and women of one generation came into contact.   Later on, when the succeeding generations were not so diverse in age, and their social separation ceased, the custom had been established, and did not lapse with the changed conditions.

There are a number of cases in which it is at least conceivable that the older customs of a people, under a new surrounding, develop into taboos.   I think, for instance, that it is very likely that the Eskimo taboo forbidding the use of caribou and of seal on the same day may be due to the alternating inland and coast life of the people. When they hunt inland, they have no seals, and consequently can eat only caribou.   When they hunt on the coast, they have no caribou, and consequently can eat only seal.   The simple fact that in one season only caribou can be eaten, and that in another season only seal can be eaten, may have easily led to a resistance to a change of this custom; so that from the fact that for a long period the two kinds of meat could not be eaten at the same time, the law developed that the two kinds of meat must not be eaten at the same time.   I think it is also likely that the fish taboo of some of our Southwestern tribes may be due to the fact that the tribes lived for a long time in a region where no fish was available, and that the impossibility of obtaining fish developed into the custom of not eating fish. These hypothetical cases make it clear that the unconscious origin of customs is quite conceivable, although of course not necessary. It seems, however, certain that even when there has been a conscious reasoning that led to the establishment of a custom, it soon ceased to be conscious, and instead we find a direct emotional resistance to an infraction of the custom.

Other actions which are considered proper or improper are continued solely through the force of habit; and no reasons are assigned for their occurrence, although the re-action against an infringement of the custom may be strong. If among the Indians of Vancouver Island it is bad form for a young woman of nobility to open her mouth wide and to eat fast, a deviation from this custom would also be deeply felt, but in this case as an impropriety which would seriously damage the social standing of the culprit. The same group of feelings are concerned when a member of the nobility, even in Europe, marries below his or her station. In other, more trifling cases, the overstepping of the boundaries of custom merely exposes the offender to ridicule, on account of the impropriety of the act.   All these cases belong psychologically to the same group of emotional re-actions against breaks with established automatic habits.

It might seem that in primitive society opportunity could hardly be given to bring into consciousness the strong emotional resistance against infractions of customs, because they are rigidly adhered to.   There is one feature of social life, however, that tends to keep the conservative attachment to customary actions before the minds of the people.   This is the education of the young. The child in whom the habitual behavior of his surroundings has not yet developed will acquire much of it by unconscious imitation.   In many cases, however, it will act in a way different from the customary manner, and will be corrected by its elders.   Any one familiar with primitive life will know that the children are constantly exhorted to follow the example of their elders, and every collection of carefully recorded traditions contains numerous references to advice given by parents to children, impressing them with the duty to observe the customs of the tribe.   The greater the emotional value of a custom, the stronger will be the desire to inculcate it in the minds of the young. Thus ample opportunity is given to bring the resistance against infractions into consciousness.

I believe that these conditions exert a very strong influence upon the development and conservation of customs; for, as soon as the breach of custom is raised into consciousness, occasions must arise when people, either led by children's questions or following their own bent to speculation, find themselves confronted with the fact that certain ideas exist for which they cannot give any explanation except that they are there. The desire to understand one's own feelings and actions, and to get a clear insight into the secrets of the world, manifests itself at a very early time, and it is therefore not surprising that man in all stages of culture begins to speculate on the motives of his own actions.

As I have explained before, there can be no conscious motive for many of these, and for this reason the tendency develops to discover the motives that may determine our customary behavior. This is the reason why, in all stages of culture, customary actions are made the subject of secondary explanations that have nothing to do with their historical origin, but which are inferences based upon the general knowledge possessed by the people.

I think the existence of such secondary interpretations of customary actions is one of the most important anthropological phenomena, and we have seen that it is hardly less common in our own society than in more primitive societies. It is a common observation that we desire or act first, and then try to justify our desires and our actions. When, on account of our early bringing-up, we act with a certain political party, most of us are not prompted by a clear conviction of the justice of the principles of our party, but we do so because we have been taught to respect it as the right party to which to belong. Then only do we justify our standpoint by trying to convince ourselves that these principles are the correct ones. Without reasoning of this kind, the stability and geographical distribution of political parties as well as of church denominations would be entirely unintelligible. A candid examination of our own minds convinces us that the average man, in by far the majority of cases, does not determine his actions by reasoning, but that he first acts, and then justifies or explains his acts by such secondary considerations as are current among us.

We have discussed so far only the class of actions in which a break with the customary brings into consciousness the emotional value of the action in question, and

releases a strong resistance to change, which is secondarily explained by certain reasons that forbid a change.
We have seen that the traditional material with which
man operates determines the particular type of explana-
tory idea that associates itself with the emotional state of
mind.   Primitive man generally bases these explanations
of his customs on concepts that are intimately related to
his general views of the constitution of the world.   Some
mythological idea may be considered the basis of a custom or of the avoidance of certain actions, or the custom
may be given a symbolic significance, or it may merely be
connected with the fear of ill luck.   Evidently this last
class of explanations is identical with those of many
superstitions that linger among us.

The essential result of this inquiry is the conclusion
that the origin of customs of primitive man must not be
looked for in rational processes.   Most investigators who
have tried to clear up the history of customs and taboos
express the view that their origin lies in speculations on
the relations between man and nature; that to primitive
man the world is filled with agencies of superhuman power,
which may harm man at the slightest provocation, and
that attempts to avoid conflict with these powers dictate
the innumerable superstitious regulations.   The impres-

sion is given that the habits and opinions of primitive man had been formed by conscious reasoning. It seems evident, however, that this whole line of thought would remain consistent if it is assumed that the processes were all subconscious.

Even granting this, I believe that these theories need extension, because it would seem that many cases of this kind may have arisen without any kind of reasoning, conscious or subconscious ; for instance, cases in which a custom became established by the general conditions of life, and came into consciousness as soon as these conditions changed. I do not doubt at all that there are cases in which customs originated by more or less conscious reasoning ; but I am just as certain that others originated without, and that our theories should cover both points.

The study of primitive life exhibits a large number of associations of a different type, which are not so easily explained. Certain patterns of associated ideas may be recognized in all types of culture.

Sombre colors and depressed feelings are closely connected in our minds, although not in those of peoples of foreign culture. Noise seems inappropriate in a place of sadness, although among primitive people the loud wail of the mourner is the natural expression of grief. Decorative art serves to please the eye, yet a design like the cross has retained its symbolic significance.

On the whole, such associations between groups of ideas apparently unrelated are rare in civilized life. That they once existed is shown by historical evidence as well as by survivals in which the old ideas have perished, although the outer form remains. In primitive culture these associations occur in great numbers. In discussing them we may begin with examples that have their analogues in our own civilization, and which therefore are readily intelligible to us.

The most extended domain of such customs is that of ritual. Accompanying important actions we find numerous stated ritual forms which are constantly applied, although their original significance has been lost entirely. Many of them are so old that their origin must be looked for in antiquity or even in prehistoric times. In our day the domain of ritual is restricted, but in primitive culture it pervades the whole life. Not a single action of any importance can be performed that is not accompanied by proscribed rites of more or less elaborate form. It has been proved in many cases that rites are more stable than their explanations; that they symbolize different ideas among different people and at different times. The diversity of rites is so great, and their occurrence so universal, that here the greatest possible variety of associations is found.

It seems to my mind that we may apply this point of view to many of the most fundamental and inexplicable traits of primitive life, and that when considered as associations between heterogeneous thoughts and activities, their rise and history become more readily intelligible.

In our modern society the consideration of cosmic phenomena is constantly associated with the efforts to give adequate explanations for them, based on the principle of causality. In primitive society the consideration of the same phenomena leads to a number of typical associations which differ from our own, but which occur with remarkable regularity among tribes living in the most remote parts of the world. An excellent instance of this kind is the regular association of observations relating to cosmic phenomena with purely human happenings; in other words, the occurrence of nature myths. It seems to my mind that the characteristic trait of nature myths is the association between the observed cosmic events and what might be called a novelistic plot based on the form of social life with which people are familiar. The plot as such might as well develop among the peoples themselves; but its association with the heavenly bodies, the thunder-storm, or the wind, makes it a nature myth. One distinction between folk-tale and nature myth lies solely in the association of the latter with cosmic phenomena. This association does not naturally develop in modern society. If it is still found every now and then, it is based on the survival of the traditional nature myth. In primitive society, on the other hand, it is found constantly. The investigation of the reason for this association is an attractive problem, the solution of which can only in part be surmised.

A number of other examples will demonstrate that the kind of association here referred to is quite common in primitive life. An excellent instance is furnished by certain characteristics of primitive decorative art. With us almost the sole object of decorative art is æsthetic. We wish to beautify the objects that are decorated. We recognize a certain appropriateness of decorative motives in accordance with the uses to which objects are to be put, and the emotional effect of the decorative motive. In primitive life the conditions are quite different. Extended investigations on decorative art in all continents have proved that practically everywhere the decorative design is associated with a certain symbolic significance. There is hardly a case known where a primitive tribe cannot give some sort of explanation for the designs in use. In some cases the symbolic significance may be exceedingly weak, but ordinarily it is highly developed. The triangular and quadrangular designs of our Plains Indians, for instance, almost always convey definite symbolic meanings. They may be records of warlike deeds, they may be prayers, or they may in some way convey other ideas relating to the supernatural. It would almost seem that among primitive tribes decorative art for its own sake does not exist. The only analogies in modern decorative art are such as the use of the flag, of the cross, or of emblems of secret societies, for decorative purposes; but their frequency is insignificant as compared to the general symbolic tendencies of primitive art. Thus it will be seen that we have here again a type of association in primitive society quite different from the type of association found among ourselves. Among primitive people the æsthetic motive is combined with the symbolic, while in modern life the æsthetic motive is either quite independent or associated with utilitarian ideas.

On the North Pacific coast of America the animal design, which is found in many other parts of the world, has associated itself firmly with the totemic idea, and has led to an unparalleled application of animal motives. This may also have helped to preserve the realistic character of this art. Among the Sioux the high valuation of military prowess, and the habit of exploiting deeds of war before the tribe, have been the causes that led the men to associate the decoration on their garments with events of war ; so that among them a military symbolism has developed, while the women of the same tribe explain the same design in an entirely different manner (Wissler). It seems to me that in this last case we have no particular difficulty in following the line of thought that leads to the association between forms of decoration and military ideas, although in general our minds require a much more conscious effort than that of primitive man. The very fact of the well-nigh universal occurrence of decorative symbolism shows that this association must establish itself automatically and without conscious reasoning.

In both mythology and art the tendency to give rationalistic explanations for the peculiar associations that have developed may be observed in those cases in which styles of art or myths are borrowed. The fact that decorative art among primitive people is almost everywhere symbolic does not preclude the possibility of designs, and even of the whole style, of one region, being borrowed from the people of another region. This has been the case, for instance, among the tribes of our Northwestern Plains, who have borrowed much of their art from their more southern neighbors; but they have not adopted at the same time its symbolical interpretations, but invented interpretations of their own. I imagine that this is the outcome of a mental process which set in when the designs were found pleasing, and, according to the general character of primitive thought, a symbolic interpretation was expected. This was then secondarily invented in accordance with the ideas current among the tribe.

The same observation may be made in primitive mythology. The same kind of tales are current over enormous areas, but the mythological use to which they are put is locally quite different. Thus an ordinary adventure relating to the exploits of some animal may sometimes be made use of to explain some of its peculiar characteristics. At other times it may be made use of to explain certain customs, or even the origin of certain constellations in the sky. There is not the slightest doubt in my mind that the tale as such is older than its mythological significance. The characteristic feature of the development of the nature myth is, first, that the tale has associated itself with attempts to explain cosmic conditions (this has been referred to before); and, secondly, that when primitive man became concious of the cosmic problem, he ransacked the entire field of his knowledge until he happened to find something that could be fitted to the problem in question, giving an explanation satisfactory to his mind.   While the classification of concepts, the types of association, and the resistance to change of automatic acts, developed unconsciously, many of the secondary explanations are due to conscious reasoning.

I will give still another example of a form of association characteristic of primitive society.   In modern society, social organization, including the grouping of families, is essentially based on blood-relationship and on the social functions performed by each individual.   Except in so far as the Church concerns itself with birth, marriage, and death, there is no connection between social organization and religious belief.   These conditions are quite different in primitive society, where we find an inextricable association of ideas and customs relating to society and to religion.   As in art form tends to associate itself with ideas entirely foreign to it, so the social unit tends to associate itself with various impressions of nature, particularly with the divisions of the animal world. This form of association seems to me the fundamental trait of totemism as found among many American tribes, as well as in Australia, Melanesia, and in Africa. I have described before its characteristic trait, which consists in a peculiar connection that is believed to exist between a certain class of objects, generally animals, and a certain social group. Further analysis shows very clearly that one of the underlying ideas of totemism is the existence of definite groups of man that are not allowed to intermarry, and that the limitations of these groups are determined by considerations of blood-relationship. The religious ideas found in totemism refer to the personal relation of man to certain classes of supernatural powers, and the typical trait of totemism is the association of certain kinds of supernatural power with certain social groups. This granted, the establishment of association with the supernatural world becomes at least intelligible. That such feelings are not by any means improbable, or even rare, is sufficiently shown by the exclusiveness of the European high nobility, or by the national emotions in their pronounced form. It is not at all difficult to understand how an overbearing enthusiasm of self-appreciation of a community may become a powerful emotion or a passion, which, on account of the lack of rational explanation of the world, will tend to associate the members of the community with all that is good and powerful. Psychologically, therefore, we may compare totemism with those familiar forms of society in which certain social classes claim privileges by the grace of God, or where the patron saint of a community favors its members with his protection. It will be recognized that we have here again a type of association in primitive society which has completely changed with the development of civilization.

However these associations may have been brought about, there is no doubt that they do exist, and that, psychologically considered, they are of the same character as those previously discussed, and that the rationalizing mind of man soon lost the historic thread, and reinterpreted the established customs in conformity with the general trend of thought of his culture. We are therefore justified in concluding that these customs must also be studied by the pragmatic method, because their present associations are not likely to be original, but rather secondary.

It is perhaps venturesome to discuss at the present moment the origin of these types of association; yet it

may be admissible to dwell on a few of the most generalized facts which seem to characterize primitive culture
as compared to civilization. ᶜFrom our point of view,
the striking features of primitive culture are the great
number of associations of entirely heterogeneous groups
of phenomena, such as natural phenomena and individual emotion, social groupings and religious concepts,
decorative art and symbolic interpretation.   These tend
to disappear with the approach to our present civilization, although a careful analysis reveals the persistence
of many, and the tendency of each automatic action to
establish its own associations according to the mental
relations in which it regularly occurs.   One of the great
changes that has taken place may perhaps best be expressed by saying that in primitive culture the impressions of the outer world are associated intimately with
subjective impressions, which they call forth regularly,
but which are determined largely by the social surroundings of the individual.   Gradually it is recognized
that these connections are more uncertain than others
that remain the same for all mankind, and in all forms
of social surroundings; and thus sets in the gradual
elimination of one subjective association after another,
which culminates in the scientific method of the present

day.   We may express this also by saying that when we
have our attention directed to a certain concept which
has a whole fringe of incident concepts related to it,
we at once associate it with that group which is represented by the category of causality.   When the same concept appears in the mind of primitive man, it associates
itself with those concepts related to it by emotional
states.

If this is true, then the associations of the primitive
mind are heterogeneous, and ours homogeneous and consistent only from our own point of view.   To the mind of
primitive man, only his own associations can be rational.
Ours must appear to him just as heterogeneous as his to
us, because the bond between the phenomena of the
world, as it appears after the elimination of their emotional associations, which is being established with increasing knowledge, does not exist for *him*, while we can
no longer feel the subjective associations that govern his
mind.

This peculiarity of association is also another expression of the conservatism of primitive culture and the
changeability of many features of our civilization.   We
tried to show that the resistance to change is largely due
to emotional sources, and that in primitive culture emo-

tional associations are the prevailing type : hence resistance against the new.   In our civilization, on the other
hand, many actions are performed merely as means to a
rational end.   They do not enter sufficiently deeply into
our minds to establish connections which would give them
emotional values : hence our readiness to change.   We
recognize, however, that we cannot remodel, without
serious emotional resistance, any of the fundamental lines
of thought and action which are determined by our early
education, and which form the subconscious basis of all
our activities.   This is evinced by the attitude of civilized
communities towards religion, politics, art, and the fundamental concepts of science.

In the average individual among primitive tribes, reasoning cannot overcome this emotional resistance, and it
therefore requires a destruction of the existing emotional
associations by more powerful means to bring about a
change., This may be effected by some event which
stirs up the mind of the people to its depths, or by economic and political changes against which resistance is
impossible.   In civilization there is a constant readiness
to modify those activities that have no emotional value.
This is true not only of activities designed to meet practical ends, but also of others that have lost their associa-

tions, and that have become subject to fashion. There remain, however, others which are retained with great tenacity, and which hold their own against reasoning, because their strength lies in their emotional values. The history of the progress of science yields example after example of the power of resistance belonging to old ideas, even after increasing knowledge of the world has undermined the ground on which they were erected. Their overthrow is not brought about until a new generation has arisen, to whom the old is no longer dear and near.

Besides this, there are a thousand activities and modes of thought that constitute our daily life, — of which we are not conscious at all until we come into contact with other types of life, or until we are prevented from acting according to our custom, — that cannot in any way be claimed to be more reasonable than others, and to which, nevertheless, we cling. These, it would seem, are hardly less numerous in civilized than in primitive culture, because they constitute the whole series of well-established habits according to which the necessary actions of ordinary every-day life are performed, and which are learned less by instruction than by imitation.

We may also express these conclusions in another

form.   While in the logical processes of the mind we find
a decided tendency, with the development of civilization,
to eliminate traditional elements, no such marked decrease in the force of traditional elements can be found
in our activities.   These are controlled by custom almost
as much among ourselves as they are among primitive
man.   We have seen why this must be the case.   The
mental processes which enter into the development of
judgments are based largely upon associations with previous judgments.   This process of association is the same
among primitive men as among civilized men, and the
difference consists largely in the modification of the
traditional material with which our new perceptions amalgamate.   In the case of activities, the conditions are somewhat different.   Here tradition manifests itself in an action performed by the individual.   The more frequently
this action is repeated, the more firmly it will become
established, and the less will be the conscious equivalent
accompanying the action ; so that customary actions
which are of very frequent repetition become entirely
unconscious.   Hand in hand with this decrease of consciousness goes an increase in the emotional value of the
omission of such activities, and still more of the performance of actions contrary to custom.   A greater will-

power is required to inhibit an action which has become well established ; and combined with this effort of the will-power are feelings of intense displeasure.

Thus an important change from primitive culture to civilization seems to consist in the gradual elimination of what might be called the social associations of sense-impressions and of activities, for which intellectual associations are gradually substituted.   This process is accompanied by a loss of conservatism, which, however, does not extend over the field of habitual activities that do not come into consciousness, and only to a slight extent over those generalizations which are the foundation of all knowledge imparted in the course of education.

IX. SUMMARY

I MAY now be allowed to pass once more briefly over the whole ground that we have covered. First of all, we tried to understand the reasons for our belief in the existence of gifted races and of others less favorably endowed, and found that it was based essentially on the assumption that higher achievement is necessarily associated with higher mental faculty, and that therefore the features of those races that in our judgment have accomplished most are characteristics of mental superiority. We subjected these assumptions to a critical study, and discovered little evidence to support them. So many other causes were found to influence the progress of civilization, accelerating or retarding it, and similar processes were active in so many different races, that, on the whole, hereditary traits, more particularly hereditary higher gifts, were at best a possible, but not a necessary, element determining the degree of advancement of a race.

The second part of the fundamental assumption seemed even less likely. Hardly any evidence could be adduced to show that the anatomical characteristics of the races possessing the highest civilization were phylogenetically more advanced than those on lower grades of culture. The various races differ in this respect; the specifically human characteristics being most highly developed, some in one race, some in another. Furthermore, it appeared that a direct relation between physical habitus and mental endowment does not exist.

After thus clearing away the racial prejudice, the most formidable obstacle to a clear understanding of our problem, we turned to an investigation of the question whether human types are stable, more particularly whether environment may change the anatomical structure of man, and thus of his mental make-up, and to the correlated question, what man owes to heredity. In treating the general question of the stability of human types, we described some rudimentary organs and some peculiar anatomical traits which prove a phylogenetic development of man, traces of which were found in all races. The influence of environment was demonstrated in all those cases in which changes in the rate of growth affected the final form of the body; and we saw particularly that early arrest of development does not necessarily mean unfavorable development, because in many cases the rapidity and short period of development seemed favorable elements. We saw that other changes in human types may be brought about by selection, and that environment itself seems to have a direct effect upon bodily form, as was proved by the changes of type due to the transfer from a rural environment to city life, and to the immigration of various nationalities from Europe to America. We saw, however, that there is no evidence at present to prove that these changes exceed certain definite limits. Special attention was directed to those features of the bodily form that characterize man as a domesticated animal, and which are due to the peculiarities of human nutrition, and which facilitate crossing of distinct types. The mentality of man appeared also to be influenced by the degree of his domestication.

Turning to the influence of heredity, we recognized that by it are determined all the most fundamental features of each race and type of man, and that often the individual reverts to the traits of the one or the other of his parents, or of his remote ancestors, in such manner that one trait may belong to one ancestor, another to another. This tendency seemed to explain the development of local types, and we recognized the importance of the breaking of old lines of heredity, in cases of intermarriages of branches of the same race that had long been separated. By analogy we concluded that possibly, or probably, similar tendencies may exist in the mental life of man.

After we had thus gained an insight into the physical characteristics of the races and social groups of man, we took up a consideration of his mental life. The mental traits common to all mankind are those which appear by contrasting man with animals; and we pointed out briefly that articulate language, the use of implements, and the power of reasoning, belong to all members of the human species as opposed to the higher animals. Before we entered into the comparison of the mental life of primitive man and of civilized man, we had to clear away a number of misconceptions caused by the current descriptions of the life of primitive man. We saw that the oft-repeated claim that he has no power to inhibit impulses, no power of attention, no originality of thought, no power of clear reasoning, could not be maintained; and that all these faculties are common to primitive man and to civilized man, although they are excited on different occasions. This led us to a brief consideration of the question whether the hereditary mental faculty was improved by civilization, an opinion that did not seem plausible to us.

The study of the problem of the relation of racial descent to cultural advancement required a determination of the question in how far these are correlated. We endeavored to gain an insight into this problem by following out the relations between human types, languages, and cultures. A general lack of correlation appeared, which led us to infer that the present types of man are older than the present linguistic families, and that each type developed a number of languages. Since these must be considered the product of the mental activities of each type, uninfluenced or almost uninfluenced by other types, we tried to discover whether one language could be shown to be superior to others, and whether some languages made higher forms of thought impossible. The results of this inquiry were quite analogous to those obtained in our inquiry into the physical characteristics of man, and showed similar traits in all languages, and also that languages were moulded by thought, not thought by languages.

There still seemed to be a possibility of proving the backwardness of certain tribes, if it could be shown that members of certain races were all on early levels of culture, while those of other races had independently reached later stages of development. This would presuppose that the general course of cultural development is the same everywhere, and that types of culture can be ascribed to definite stages of development. The theory of such general parallelism of the history of human culture is based on the similarity of cultural traits in all parts of the world. Our analysis showed that the similarities were more apparent than real, that they often developed by convergent development from distinct sources, and that not all stages have been present in all types of cultures. Thus all attempts to correlate racial types and cultural stages failed us, and we concluded that cultural stage is essentially a phenomenon dependent upon historical causes, regardless of race.

Finally we attempted to describe the mental characteristics of primitive man, regardless of his racial affiliations. We pointed out the differences in principles of classification of experience found on different social stages, and the differences in logical conclusions reached by primitive and civilized man owing to the difference in the character of knowledge accumulated by preceding generations. We then followed out the emotional associations of habitual activities, and the tendency to invent for them rationalistic explanations. We found them quite common in primitive life, and noticed the great variety of ideas and activities that were thus brought into contact so as to produce a number of peculiar concepts and activities. Other peculiar associations are not due to strong emotional causes, but to all of them is common the tendency of taking on rationalistic explanations of varied character. The change from primitive to civilized society includes a lessening of the number of the emotional associations, and an improvement of the traditional material that enters into our habitual mental operations.

X. RACE PROBLEMS IN THE UNITED STATES

WE will now turn to the question what these results of our inquiry teach us in regard to the problems that confront our modern civilization, particularly our nation. The development of the American nation through the amalgamation of diverse European nationalities, the presence of the Negro, Indian, and Chinese, and the whole ever-increasing heterogeneity of the component elements of our people, involve a number of problems to the solution of which our inquiries contribute important data.

Our previous considerations make clear the hypothetical character of many of the generally accepted assumptions, and indicate that not all of the questions involved can be answered at the present time with scientific accuracy. It is disappointing that we have to take this critical attitude, because the political question of dealing with all these groups of people is of great and immediate importance. However, it should be solved on the basis of scientific knowledge, not according to emotional clamor. Under present conditions, we seem to be called upon to formulate definite answers to questions that require the most painstaking and unbiassed investigation; and the more urgent the demand for final conclusions, the more needed is a critical examination of the phenomena and of the available methods of solution.

Let us first represent to our minds the facts relating to the origins of our nation. When British immigrants first flocked to the Atlantic coast of North America, they found a continent inhabited by Indians. The population of the country was thin, and vanished comparatively rapidly before the influx of the more numerous Europeans. The settlement of the Dutch on the Hudson, of the Germans in Pennsylvania, not to speak of other nationalities, is familiar to all of us. We know that the foundations of our modern state were laid by Spaniards in the Southwest, by French in the Mississippi Basin and in the region of the Great Lakes, but that the British immigration far outnumbered that of other nationalities. In the composition of our people, the indigenous element has never played an important role, except for very short periods. In regions where the settlement progressed for a long time entirely by the immigration of unmarried males of the white race, families of mixed blood have been of some importance during the period of gradual development, but they have never become sufficiently numerous in any populous part of the United States to be considered as an important element in our population. Without any doubt, Indian blood flows in the veins of quite a number of our people, but the proportion is so insignificant that it may well be disregarded.

Much more important has been the introduction of the negro, whose numbers have increased many fold, so that they form now about one-eighth of our whole nation. For a certain length of time the immigration of Asiatic nations seemed likely to become of importance in the development of our country, but the political events of recent years have tended to decrease their immediate importance considerably, although we do not venture to predict that the relation of Asiatics and white Americans may not become a most important problem in the future. These facts, however, are familiar to all of us, and stand out clearly to our minds.

More recent is the problem of the immigration of people representing all the nationalities of Europe, western Asia, and northern Africa. While until late in the second half of the nineteenth century the immigrants consisted almost entirely of people of northwestern Europe, natives of Great Britain, Scandinavia, Germany, Switzerland, Holland, Belgium, and France, the composition of the immigrant masses has changed completely since that time. With the economic development of Germany, German immigration has dwindled down; while at the same time Italians, the various Slavic peoples of Austria, Russia, and the Balkan Peninsula, Hungarians, Roumanians, East European Hebrews, not to mention the numerous other nationalities, have arrived in ever increasing numbers. There is no doubt that these people of eastern and southern Europe represent physical types distinct from the physical type of northwestern Europe; and it is clear, even to the most casual observer, that their present social standards differ fundamentally from our own. Since the number of new arrivals may be counted in normal years by hundreds of thousands, the question may well be asked, What will be the result of this influx of types distinct from our own, if it is to continue for a considerable length of time?

It is often claimed that the phenomenon of mixture presented in the United States is unique; that a similar intermixture has never occurred before in the world's history; and that our nation is destined to become what some writers choose to term a "mongrel" nation in a sense that has never been equalled anywhere.

When we try to analyze the phenomenon in greater detail, and in the light of our knowledge of conditions in Europe as well as in other continents, this view does not seem to me tenable. In speaking of European types, we are accustomed to consider them as, comparatively speaking, pure stocks. It is easy to show that this view is erroneous. It is only necessary to look at a map illustrating the racial types of any European country — like Italy, for instance — to see that local divergence is the characteristic feature, uniformity of type the exception. Thus Dr. Ridolfo Livi, in his fundamental investigations on the anthropology of Italy, has shown that the types of the extreme north and of the extreme south are quite distinct, — the former tall, short-headed, with a considerable sprinkling of blond and blue-eyed individuals; the latter short, long-headed, and remarkably dark. The transition from one type to the other is, on the whole, quite gradual; but, like isolated islands, distinct types occur here and there. The region of Lucca in Tuscany, and the district of Naples, are examples of this kind, which may be explained as due to the survival of an older

stock, to the intrusion of new types, or to a peculiar influence of environment.

Historical evidence is quite in accord with the results
derived from the investigation of the distribution of
modern types. In the earliest times we find on the peninsula of Italy groups of heterogeneous people, the linguistic relationships of many of which have remained
obscure up to the present time. From the earliest prehistoric times on, we see wave after wave of people invading
Italy from the north. Very early Greeks settled in the
greater part of southern Italy, and Phœnician influence
was well established on the west coast of the peninsula.
A lively intercourse existed between Italy and northern
Africa. Slaves of Berber blood were imported, and have
left their traces. Slave trade continued to bring new
blood into the country until quite recent times, and Livi
believes that he can trace the type of Crimean slaves who
were introduced late in the middle ages in the region of
Venice. In the course of the centuries, the migrations
of Celtic and Teutonic tribes, the conquests of the Nor-
mans, the contact with Africa, have added their share to
the mixture of people on the Italian peninsula.

The fates of other parts of Europe were no less diversi-
fied. The Pyrenæan Peninsula, which at present seems

to be one of the most isolated parts of Europe, had a most checkered history. The earliest inhabitants of whom we know were presumably related to the Basques of the Pyrenees. These were subjected to Oriental influences in the pre-Mycenæan period, to Punic influences, to Celtic invasions, Roman colonization, Teutonic invasions, the Moorish conquest, and later on to the peculiar selective process that accompanied the driving-out of the Moors and the Jews.

England was not exempt from vicissitudes of this kind. It seems plausible that at a very early period the type which is now found principally in Wales and in some parts of Ireland occupied the greater portion of the islands. It was swamped by successive waves of Celtic, Roman, and Anglo-Saxon migration. Thus we find change everywhere.

The history of the migrations of the Goths, the invasions of the Huns, who in the short interval of one century moved their habitations from the borders of China into the very centre of Europe, are proofs of the enormous changes in population that have taken place in early times.

Slow colonization has also brought about fundamental changes in blood as well as in diffusion of languages and cultures. Perhaps the most striking recent example of this change is presented by the gradual Germanization of the region east of the Elbe River, where, after the Teutonic migrations, people speaking Slavic languages had settled. The gradual absorption of Celtic communities, of the Basque, in ancient times the great Roman colonization, and later the Arab conquest of North Africa, are examples of similar processes.

Intermixture in early times was not by any means confined to peoples which, although diverse in language and culture, were of fairly uniform type. On the contrary, the most diverse types of southern Europe, northern Europe, eastern Europe, and western Europe, not to mention the elements which poured into Europe from Asia and Africa, have been participants in this long-continued intermixture.

There is, however, one fundamental difference in regard to the early European migrations and the modern transatlantic migration. On the whole, the former took place at a period when the density of population was, comparatively speaking, small. There is no doubt that the number of individuals concerned in the formation of the modern types of Great Britain were comparatively few as compared with the millions who come together to form a new nation in the United States; and it is obvious that the process of amalgamation which takes place in communities that must be counted by millions differs in character from the process of amalgamation that takes place in communities that may be counted by thousands. Setting aside social barriers, which in early times as well as now undoubtedly tended to keep intermingling peoples separate, it would seem that in the more populous communities of modern times a greater permanence of the single combining elements might occur, owing to their larger numbers, which make the opportunities for segregation more favorable.

Among the smaller communities the process of amalgamation must have been an exceedingly rapid one. After the social distinctions have once been obliterated, pure descendants of one of the component types decrease greatly in number, and the fourth generation of a people consisting originally of distinct elements will be almost homogeneous. I shall revert to this phenomenon later on.

It might be objected to this point of view, that the very diversity of local types in Europe proves the homogeneity of race types, — as, for instance, of the north-western European type, the Mediterranean type, the East

European type, or the Alpine type, — but it must be remembered that we have historical proof of the process of mixture, and that the relative number of component elements is sufficient to account for the present conditions.

I think we may dismiss the assumption of the existence of a pure type in any part of Europe, and of a process of mongrelization in America different from anything that has taken place for thousands of years in Europe. Neither are we right in assuming that the phenomenon is one of a more rapid intermixture than the one prevailing in olden times. The difference is based essentially in the masses of individuals concerned in the process.

If we confine our consideration for the present to the intermixture of European types in America, I think it will be clear, from what has been said before, that the concern that is felt by many in regard to the continuance of racial purity of our nation is to a great extent imaginary. The history of Europe proves that there has been no racial purity anywhere for exceedingly long periods, neither has the continued intermixture of European types shown any degrading effect upon any of the European nationalities. It would be just as easy to prove that those nations that have been least disturbed have lacked the stimulus to further advance, and have passed through periods of quiescence. The history of Spain might be interpreted as an instance of an occurrence of this kind.

The question as to the actual effects of intermixture will not, however, be answered by a generalized historical treatment such as we have attempted here. The advocates of the theory of a degradation of type by the influx of so-called "lower" types, will not be silenced by reference to earlier mixtures in Europe, the course of which can no longer be traced in actual detail; for we do not know to what extent actual intermarriages have taken place, and what the development of families of mixed descent as compared with those of pure descent has been. It seems necessary that the problem should be approached from a biological standpoint. It has seemed well, however, to gain first a clearer view of the historical relations of our problem. A knowledge of the events of the past tends to lay our apprehensions, that make the problem exciting, and which for this reason fill the observer with a strong bias for the results which he fears or desires.

Two questions stand out prominently in the study of the physical characteristics of the immigrant population. The first is the question of the influence of selection and environment in the migration from Europe to America.

The second is the question of the influence of inter-mixture.

We have been able to throw some light upon both of these.

We found that the types which come to our shores do not remain stable, but show such important modifications, that many of the differences of the human types of Europe seem rather ephemeral than permanent, determined more by environment than by heredity. The characteristics which belong to the influences of environment belong to the most fundamental traits of the body. Stature, form of head, and size of face, seem to be equally subject to these influences; and the modifications are the more marked, the less developed the organ in question at the time of birth, the longer it is therefore subject to the influences of environment. This fact allows us to assert with a high degree of confidence that mental traits as well as physical traits will be modified by the effect of environment. When, furthermore, we recall that we could not discover any proofs of the superiority of one type over another, we may feel safe when we state that the dangers to the vigor of the American nation, due to an influx of alien European types, is imaginative, not real.

A number of data have also been obtained for a better

understanding of the significance of race-mixture. Let us recall that one of the most powerful agents modifying human types is the breaking-up of the continuance of certain strains in small communities by a process of rapid migration, which occurs both in Europe and in America, but with much greater rapidity in our country, because the heterogeneity of descent of the people is much greater than in the countries of Europe.

What effect these processes may have upon the ultimate type and variability of the American people cannot be determined at the present time ; but no evidence is available that would allow us to expect a lower status of the developing new types of America. Much remains to be done in the study of this subject ; and, considering our lack of knowledge of the most elementary facts that determine the outcome of this process, I feel that it behooves us to be most cautious in our reasoning, and particularly to refrain from all sensational formulations of the problem that are liable to add to the prevalent lack of calmness in its consideration ; the more so, since the answer to these questions concerns the welfare of millions of people.

The problem is one in regard to which speculation is as easy as accurate studies are difficult. Basing our argu-

ments on ill-fitting analogies with the animal and plant
world, we may speculate on the effects of intermixture
upon the development of new types — as though the mixture that is taking place in America were in any sense,
except a sociological one, different from the mixtures
that have taken place in Europe for thousands of years;
looking for a general degradation, for reversion to remote
ancestral types, or towards the evolution of a new ideal
type — as fancy or personal inclination may impel us.
We may enlarge on the danger of the impending sub-
mergence of the northwest European type, or glory in the
prospect of its dominance over all others.   Would it not
be a safer course to investigate the truth or fallacy of each
theory rather than excite the public mind by indulgence
in the fancies of our speculation ?   That these are an important help in the attainment of truth, I do not deny;
but they must not be promulgated before they have been
subjected to a searching analysis, lest the credulous
public mistake fancy for truth.

If I am not in a position to predict what the effect of
mixture of distinct types may be, I feel confident that this
important problem may be solved if it is taken up with
sufficient energy and on a sufficiently large scale.   An
investigation of the anthropological data of people of dis-

tinct types, — taking into consideration the similarities and dissimilarities of parents and children, the rapidity and final result of the physical and mental development of children, their vitality, the fertility of marriages of different types and in different social strata, — such an investigation is bound to give us information which will allow us to answer these important questions definitely and conclusively.

The final result of race-mixture will necessarily depend upon the fertility of the present native population and of the newer immigrants. It has been pointed out repeatedly that the birth-rate of Americans has declined with great rapidity, and that in the second and third generations of descendants of immigrants the same decline makes itself felt. It will therefore be important to know what the fertility of different types may be.

If the fertility of foreigners continues high without a correspondingly higher death-rate of children, we may anticipate a gradual increase of the physical influence of the more fertile type. The immigration of the divergent types of southern and eastern Europe is, however, so recent, that this question cannot be answered until at least twenty years more have elapsed.

No less important than the fertility of each immigrant

type by itself is the question in how far they tend to intermarry.   The data presented in our census reports do not
give a clear insight into this tendency among various nationalities.   The difficulties of collecting significant statistics on the problem are very great.   They appear particularly clearly in the case of Italians.   Married men from
Italy come to the United States, earn some money, and
go back to rejoin their families.   They may come again,
and, when conditions are propitious, they may finally
send for their families to follow them.   Thus we find
among the Italian immigrants very large numbers who
were married before they came here.   It seems almost
impossible to separate the contingent of couples married
before their arrival here from those married after
their arrival, and the chief point of interest to us lies
in the intermarriages of children born in this country.
It is natural that in large cities, where nationalities separate in various quarters, a great amount of cohesion
should continue for some time; but it seems likely that
intermarriages between descendants of foreign nationalities are much more common than the census figures would
make it appear.   Our experience with Americans whose
grandparents immigrated into this country is, on the
whole, that most social traces of their descent have dis-

appeared, and that many do not even know to what nationalities their grandparents belonged. It might be expected — particularly in Western communities, where a rapid change of location is common — that this would result in a rapid mixture of the descendants of various nationalities. This inquiry, which it is quite feasible to carry out in detail, seems indispensable for a clear understanding of the situation.

It is somewhat difficult to realize how rapidly intermixture of distinct types takes place if the choice of mates is left entirely to accident. I have made this calculation, and I find that in a population in which two types intermingle, and in which both types occur with equal frequency, there will be in the fourth generation less than one person in ten thousand of pure descent. When the proportion of the two original types is as eight to one, there will be among the more numerous part of the population less than thirty in one thousand in the fourth generation that will be of pure blood. Taking these data as a basis, it is obvious that intermixture, as soon as the social barriers have been removed, must be exceedingly rapid; and I think it safe to assume that one hundred years from now, in the bulk of our population, very few pure descendants of the present immigrants will be found.

Unfortunately, however, we do not know the influence of racial cohesion. Obviously this is one of the fundamental points that ought to be known in order to gain a clear insight into the effect of recent immigration. Without this information, the whole discussion of the effect of intermixture remains speculative. The results of the present census will give us a certain amount of much-needed information on these points.

In these remarks on the problems of European immigration I have confined myself entirely to the biological problem, because all our considerations have shown conclusively that mental life is so plastic, that no hereditary inability can be assumed to exist in any of the peoples of Europe.

When we turn our attention to the negro problem as it presents itself in the United States, we must remember our previous considerations, in which we found that no proof of an inferiority of the negro type could be given, except that it seemed possible that perhaps the race would not produce quite so many men of highest genius as other races, while there was nothing at all that could be interpreted as suggesting any material difference in the mental capacity of the bulk of the negro population as compared to the bulk of the white population.

Much has been said about the shorter period of growth of the negro child as compared to the white child, but no convincing data have been forthcoming. Considering the great variation in the duration of growth and development in different individuals and in various social classes, according to the more or less favorable nutrition of the child, the information that we possess in regard to the negro child is practically without value. We have not even evidence that would prove that a shorter period of development must be unfavorable in its results. Neither do we know at what period and in what manner develop the typical negroid features, which are much less pronounced in the new-born than in adults.

It is surprising, that, notwithstanding their importance, no attempts have been made to gain a better insight into these anatomical and physiological problems, some of which might be solved without much difficulty. As it is, almost all we can say with certainty is, that the differences between the average types of the white and of the negro, that have a bearing upon vitality and mental ability, are much less than the individual variations in each race.

This result is, however, of great importance, and is quite in accord with the result of ethnological observation.

A survey of African tribes exhibits to our view cultural achievements of no mean order. To those unfamiliar with the products of native African art and industry, a walk through one of the large museums of Europe would be a revelation. None of our American museums has made collections that exhibit this subject in any way worthily. The blacksmith, the wood-carver, the weaver, the potter, — these all produce ware original in form, executed with great care, and exhibiting that love of labor, and interest in the results of work, which are apparently so often lacking among the negroes in our American surroundings. No less instructive are the records of travellers, reporting the thrift of the native villages, of the extended trade of the country, and of its markets. The power of organization as illustrated in the government of native states is of no mean order, and when wielded by men of great personality has led to the foundation of extended empires. All the different kinds of activities that we consider valuable in the citizens of our country may be found in aboriginal Africa. Neither is the wisdom of the philosopher absent. A perusal of any of the collections of African proverbs that have been published will demonstrate the homely practical philosophy of the negro, which is often proof of sound feeling and judgment.

It would be out of place to enlarge on this subject, because the essential point that anthropology can contribute to the practical discussion of the adaptability of the negro is a decision of the question how far the undesirable traits that are at present undoubtedly found in our negro population are due to racial traits, and how far they are due to social surroundings for which we are responsible. To this question anthropology can give the decided answer that the traits of African culture as observed in the aboriginal home of the negro are those of a healthy primitive people, with a considerable degree of personal initiative, with a talent for organization, and with imaginative power, with technical skill and thrift. Neither is a warlike spirit absent in the race, as is proved by the mighty conquerors who overthrew states and founded new empires, and by the courage of the armies that follow the bidding of their leaders. There is nothing to prove that licentiousness, shiftless laziness, lack of initiative, are fundamental characteristics of the race. Everything points out that these qualities are the result of social conditions rather than of hereditary traits.

It may be well to state here once more with some emphasis that it would be erroneous to assume that there are no differences in the mental make-up of the negro race and of other races, and that their activities should run in the same lines. On the contrary, if there is any meaning in correlation of anatomical structure and physiological function, we must expect that differences exist. There is, however, no evidence whatever that would stigmatize the negro as of weaker build, or as subject to inclinations and powers that are opposed to our social organization. An unbiassed estimate of the anthropological evidence so far brought forward does not permit us to countenance the belief in a racial inferiority which would unfit an individual of the negro race to take his part in modern civilization. We do not know of any demand made on the human body or mind in modern life that anatomical or ethnological evidence would prove to be beyond the powers of the negro.

The traits of the American negro are adequately explained on the basis of his history and social status. The tearing-away from the African soil and the consequent complete loss of the old standards of life, which were replaced by the dependency of slavery and by all it entailed, followed by a period of disorganization and by a severe economic struggle against heavy odds, are sufficient to explain the inferiority of the status of the race, without falling back upon the theory of hereditary inferiority.

In short, there is every reason to believe that the negro, when given facility and opportunity, will be perfectly able to fulfil the duties of citizenship as well as his white neighbor. It may be that he will not produce as many great men as the white race, and that his average achievement will not quite reach the level of the average achievement of the white race ; but there will be endless numbers who will be able to outrun their white competitors, and who will do better than the defectives whom we permit to drag down and to retard the healthy children of our public schools.

The anthropological discussion of the negro problem requires also a word on the "race instinct" of the whites, which plays a most important part in the practical aspect of the problem. Ultimately this phenomenon is a repetition of the old instinct and fear of the connubium of patricians and plebeians, of the European nobility and the common people, or of the castes of India. The emotions and reasonings concerned are the same in every respect. In our case they relate particularly to the necessity of maintaining a distinct social status in order to avoid race-mixture. As in the other cases mentioned, the so-called instinct is not a physiological dislike. This is proved by the existence of our large mulatto population, as well as by the more ready amalgamation of the Latin peoples. It is rather an expression of social conditions that are so deeply ingrained in us that they assume a strong emotional value; and this, I presume, is meant when we call such feelings instinctive. The feeling certainly has nothing to do with the question of the vitality and ability of the mulatto.

Still the questions of race-mixture and of the negro's adaptability to our environment represent a number of important problems.

I think we have reason to be ashamed to confess that the scientific study of these questions has never received the support either of our government or of any of our great scientific institutions; and it is hard to understand why we are so indifferent toward a question which is of paramount importance to the welfare of our nation. The anatomy of the American negro is not well known; and, notwithstanding the oft-repeated assertions regarding the hereditary inferiority of the mulatto, we know hardly anything on this subject. If his vitality is lower than that of the full-blooded negro, this may be as much due to social causes as to hereditary causes. Owing to the very large number of mulattoes in our country, it would not be a difficult matter to investigate the biological aspects of this question thoroughly. The importance of researches on this subject cannot be too strongly urged, since the desirability or undesirability of race-mixture should be known. Looking into a distant future, it seems reasonably certain that with the increasing mobility of the negro, the number of full-bloods will rapidly decrease ; and since there is no introduction of new negro blood, there cannot be the slightest doubt that the ultimate effect of the contact between the two races must necessarily be a continued increase of the amount of white blood in the negro community.

This process will go on most rapidly inside of the colored community, owing to intermarriages between mulattoes and full-blooded negroes. Whether or not the addition of white blood to the colored population is sufficiently large to counterbalance this levelling effect, which will make the mixed bloods with a slight strain of negro blood darker, is difficult to tell ; but it is quite obvious that, although our laws may retard the influx of white blood considerably, they cannot hinder the gradual progress of intermixture. If the powerful caste system of India has not been able to prevent intermixture, our laws, which recognize a greater amount of individual liberty, will certainly not be able to do so ; and that there is no racial sexual antipathy is made sufficiently clear by the size of our mulatto population. A candid considera- tion of the manner in which intermixture takes place shows very clearly that the probability of the infusion of white blood into the colored population is considerable. While the large body of the white population will always. at least for a very long time to come, be entirely remote from any possibility of intermixture with negroes, I think that we may predict with a fair degree of certainty a condition in which the contrast between colored people and whites will be less marked than it is at the present time. Notwithstanding all the obstacles that may be laid in the way of intermixture, the conditions are such that the persistence of the pure negro type is practically impossible. Not even an excessively high mortality and lack of fertility among the mixed type, as compared with the pure types, could prevent this result. Since it is impossible to change these conditions, they should be faced squarely, and we ought to demand a careful and critical investigation of the whole problem.

It seems to my mind that the policy of many of our Southern States that try to prevent all racial intermix- ture is based on an erroneous view of the process involved. The alleged reason for this type of legislation is the necessity of protecting the white race against the infusion of negro blood. As a matter of fact, this danger does not exist. With very few exceptions, the unions between whites and negroes are those of white men and negro women. The increase of races, however, is such that the number of children born does not depend upon the number of men, but upon the number of women. Given, therefore, a certain number of negro women, the increase of the colored population will depend upon their number; and if a considerable number of their children are those of white fathers, the race as a whole must necessarily lose its pure negro type. At the same time no such infusion of negro blood into the white race through the maternal line occurs, so that the process is actually one of lightening the negro race without corresponding admixture in the white race.

It appears from this consideration that the most important practical questions relating to the negro problem have reference to the mulattoes and other mixed bloods, — to their physical types, their mental and moral qualities, and their vitality. When the bulky literature of this subject is carefully sifted, little remains that will endure serious criticism; and I do not believe that I claim too much when I say that the whole work on this subject remains to be done. The development of modern methods of research makes it certain that by careful inquiry definite answers to our problems may be found. Is it not, then, our plain duty to inform ourselves, that, so far as that can be done, deliberate consideration of observations may take the place of heated discussion of beliefs in matters that concern not only ourselves, but also the welfare of millions of negroes?

I hope the discussions contained in these pages have shown that the data of anthropology teach us a greater tolerance of forms of civilization different from our own, and that we should learn to look upon foreign races with greater sympathy, and with the conviction, that, as all races have contributed in the past to cultural progress in one way or another, so they will be capable of advancing the interests of mankind, if we are only willing to give them a fair opportunity.

NOTES

Page 8.

A general presentation of these data will be found in F. RATZEL, History of Mankind; SOPHUS MULLER, Urgeschichte Europas.

Page 9.

A. PENCK, "Das Alter des Menschengeschlechtes" (*Zeitschrift fur Ethnologie*, vol. xl, pp. 390 *et seq.*); PENCK AND BRUCKNER, Die Alpen im Eiszeitalter (Leipzig).

Page 10.

TH. WAITZ, Anthropologie der Naturvolker (2d ed.), vol. i, p. 381.

Page 13.

GEORG GERLAND, Das Aussterben der Naturvolker; F. RATZEL, Anthropogeographie, vol. ii, pp. 330 *et seq.*

Page 14.

1. HENRY BARTH, Travels and Discoveries in North and Central Africa (2d ed., London, 1857–1858), vol. ii, pp. 253 *et seq.;* vol. iii, pp. 425 *et seq.*, 528 *et seq.;* vol. iv, pp. 406 *et seq.*, 579 *et seq.*

2. GUSTAV NACHTIGAL, Sahara und Sudan, vol. ii, pp. 391 *et seq.*, 691 *et seq.;* vol. iii, pp. 270 *et seq.*, 355 *et seq.*

Page 16.

MARY WHITE OVINGTON, Half a Man, the Status of the Negro in New York (New York, Longmans, Green, and Co., 1911).

Page 18.

1. ROBERT BENNETT BEAN, "On a Racial Peculiarity in the Brain of the Negro" (*American Journal of Anatomy*, vol. iv [1905]).

2. Fr. P. MALL, "On Several Anatomical Characters of the Human Brain, said to vary according to Race and Sex, etc." (*Ibid.*, vol. ix, pp. 1-32).

Page 21.

1. H. KLAATSCH, "The Skull of the Australian Aboriginal" (*Reports from the Pathological Laboratory of the Lunacy Department, New South Wales Government*, vol. i, part iii [Sydney, 1908], pp. 3-167); "Der primitive Mensch der Vergangenheit und Gegenwart" (*Verhandlungen der Gesellschaft deutscher Naturforscher und Aerzte*, 80 Vers. zu Coln, part i, p. 95); Anatomische Hefte, 1902.

2. C. H. STRATZ DEN HAAG, "Das Problem der Rasseneinteilung der Menschheit" (*Archiv fur Anthropologie*, N. S., vol. i, pp. 189 *et seq.*).

3. OTTO SCHOETENSACK, "Die Bedeutung Australiens fur die Heranbildung des Menschen aus einer niederen Form" (*Zeitschrift fur Ethnologie*, vol. xxxiii [1901], pp. 127 *et seq.*).

4. D. J. CUNNINGHAM, "The Lumbar Curve in Man and Apes" (*Cunningham Memoirs* [Dublin, 1886]).

Page 24.

1. KARL PEARSON, "On the Relationship of Intelligence to Size and Shape of Head, and to other Physical and Mental Characters" (*Biometrika*, vol. v, pp. 136 *et seq.*).

2. L. MANOUVRIER, "Les aptitudes et les actes dans leurs rapports avec la constitution anatomique et avec le milieu exterieur" (*Bulletins de la Societe d'Anthropologie de Paris*, 4° series, vol. i [1800], pp. 918 *et seq.*).

Page 25.

P. TOPINARD, Élements d'Anthropologie generale, p. 620. The

value for African negroes is here very small. Another
series quoted by Topinard (*Ibid.*, p. 622), consisting of
100 skulls of each group, gives the following averages:
Parisians, 1551 cc.; Auvergnats, 1585 cc.; African negroes, 1477 cc.; New Caledonians, 1488 cc. (a misprint in
Topinard's book makes this appear as 1588 cc.).

Page 26.

1. L. MANOUVRIER, "Sur l'interpretation de la quantité dans
   l'encephale" (*Memoires de la Societe d'Anthropologie de
   Paris*, 2d series, vol. iii, pp. 284, 277, 281).
2. F. GALTON, "Head Growth in Students at Cambridge"
   (*Journal of the Anthropological Institute of Great Britain
   and Ireland*, vol. xviii, p. 156).

Page 27.

A. DA COSTA FERRAIRA, "La capacite du crane chez les Portugais"
(*Bulletins et Memoires de la Societe d'Anthropologie de
Paris*, Serie V, vol. iv [1903], pp. 417 *et seq.*).

Page 28.

H. H. DONALDSON, The Growth of the Brain (1895); RAYMOND
PEARL, "Variation and Correlation in Brain-Weight"
(*Biometrika*, vol. iv, pp. 13 *et seq.*).

Page 29.

FRANKLIN P. MALL. See note 2 to p. 18.

Page 36.

R. H. LOCK, Recent Progress in the Study of Variation, Heredity
and Evolution (1006), pp. 73 *et seq.;* A. L. BOWLEY,
Elements of Statistics (1901).

Page 41.

R. WIEDERSHEIM, Der Bau des Menschen (4th ed., 1908);
The Structure of Man an Index to his Past History
(1895).

Page 44.

J. KOLLMANN, "Beiträge zur einer Kraniologie der Europäischen
Volker" (*Archiv fur Anthropologie*, vol. xiii; vol. xiv, pp.
1, 79, 179); "Die Rassenanatomie der Hand und die
Persistenz der Rassenmerkmale" (*Ibid.*, vol. xxviii, pp. 91
et seq.).

Page 45.

1. J. DENIKER, The Races of Man.
2. B. A. GOULD, Investigations in the Military and Anthropological Statistics of American Soldiers (New York, 1869);
   J. H. BAXTER, Statistics, Medical and Anthropological
   (Washington, 1875).
3. H. P. BOWDITCH, "The Growth of Children" (*Eighth Annual
   Report of the State Board of Health of Massachusetts* [Bos-
   ton, 1877]).
4. GEO. W. PECKHAM, "The Growth of Children" (*Sixth Annual
   Report of the State Board of Health of Wisconsin*).
5. OTTO AMMON, Zur Anthropologie der Badener (Jena, 1899),
   p. 514; EDV. PH. MACKEPRANG, "De Varnepligtiger Le-
   gemshøjde i Danmark" (*Meddelelser om Danmarks An-
   tropologi* [Kopenhagen, 1907], vol. i); HANS DAAE, Lege-
   mets udvikling hos Norges mandlige ungdom.

Page 46.

WILLIAM Z. RIPLEY, The Races of Europe (New York, 1899),
p. 381.

Page 48.

1. For general data on growth see S. Weissenberg, Das Wachs-
   tum des Menschen (1911).
2. F. BOAS and C. WISSLER, Statistics of Growth (*Report of the
   U.S. Commissioner of Education for 1904*, pp. 25-132).

Page 49.

E. MEUMANN, Vorlesungen zur Einführung in die experimentelle
Padagogik (Leipzig, 1907), vol. i.

Page 50.

1. RIEGER, Ueber die Beziehungen der Schadellehre zu Psychologie, Psychiatrie und Ethnologie (1882).
2. JOSEPH ENGEL, Untersuchungen über Schadelformen (Prag, 1851).
3. G. WALCHER, "Ueber die Entstehung von Brachy- und Dolichokephalie" (*Zentralblatt fur Gynakologie*, vol. xxix [1904], No. 7); see also ANTON NYSTRÖM, "Ueber die Formenveränderungen des menschlichen Schädels und deren Ursachen" (*Archiv fur Anthropologie*, vol. xxvii, pp. 211 *et seq.*).
4. OTTO AMMON, Zur Anthropologie der Badener (Jena, 1899), p. 641; Die natürliche Auslese beim Menschen (1893); see also DE LAPOUGE, "Recherches sur l'anthropologie de l'Ille-et-Vilaine" (*Bulletin de la Societe scientifique et medicale de l'Ouest* [Rennes, 1895]).

Page 51.

1. RIDOLFO LIVI, Antropometria Militare (Rome, 1896), pp. 87 *et seq.*
2. F. C. SHRUBSALL, "Physical Characters and Morbid Proclivities" (*St. Bartholomew's Hospital Reports*, 1904, vol. xxxix, pp. 63 *et seq.*).

Page 52.

See, for instance, W. Z. RIPLEY, The Races of Europe (New York, 1899).

Page 53.

FRANZ BOAS, Changes in Bodily Form of Descendants of Immigrants, being partial report on the results of an anthropological investigation for the U.S. Immigration Commission (Senate Document No. 208, 61st Congress, 2d session, Washington, 1910); Abstract of the Report on Changes in Bodily Form of Descendants of Immigrants (Washington, 1911).

Page 59.

WALCHER. See note 3 to p. 50.

Page 60.

F. BOAS, "The Cephalic Index" (*American Anthropologist*, N. S., vol. i, pp. 448 *et seq.*).

Page 65.

GUSTAV FRITSCH, Die Eingeborenen Süd-Afrikas (Breslau, 1872), pp. 30 *et seq.*

Page 68.

1. C. KELLER, "Die Haustiere als menschlicher Kulturerwerb" (*Der Mensch und die Erde* [Berlin, 1906], vol. i, pp. 165–304); Naturgeschichte der Haustiere (Berlin, 1905). STUDER, Die prahistorischen Hunde in ihrer Beziehung zu den gegenwartig lebenden Rassen (Zurich, 1901).

2. BECKMANN, Geschichte und Beziehung der Rassen der Hunde (Brunswick, 1894–95).

Page 69.

W. BOGORAS, The Chukchee (Publications of the Jesup North Pacific Expedition [Leyden, 1904–1909], vol. vii, pp. 73 *et seq.*). Compare, however, J. A. ALLEN, "Report on the Mammals collected in Northeast Siberia by the Jesup North Pacific Expedition" (*Bulletin American Museum of Natural History* [New York, 1903], vol. xix, p. 126).

Page 73.

1. K. PEARSON, "Mathematical Contributions to the Theory of Evolution, III" (*Philosophical Transactions*, 1896–97, pp. 253 *et seq.*).

2. H. H. RISLEY and E. A. GAIT, Census of India, 1901 (Calcutta, 1903), vol. i, pp. 489 *et seq.*

Page 74.

1. G. NACHTIGAL, Sahăra und Sudan, vol. ii, pp. 424 *et seq.*

2. RUDOLF MARTIN, Die Inlandstamme der Malayischen Halbinsel (Jena, 1905), pp. 1011–1012.

Page 77.

FRANCIS GALTON, Natural Inheritance. KARL PEARSON, "Law of Ancestral Heredity" (*Proceedings of the Royal Society of London*, vol. lxii, pp. 387, 388); "Law of Reversion" (*Ibid.*, vol. lxvi, pp. 142 *et seq.*); "On a Criterion which may serve to test Various Theories of Inheritance" (*Zeitschrift fur Morphologie und Anthropologie*, vol. vii [1904], pp. 524 *et seq.*).

Page 78.

1. R. H. LOCK, Recent Progress in the Study of Variation, Heredity and Evolution (1906); BATESON, Mendelism.

2. FRANZ BOAS, "Zur Anthropologie der nordamerikanischen Indianer" (*Verhandlungen der Berliner Gesellschaft für Anthropologie, Ethnologie u. Urgeschichte*, vol. xxvii [1895], pp. 366 *et seq.*); "The Half-Blood Indian" (*Popular Science Monthly*, vol. xlv [1894], pp. 761 *et seq.*).

Page 80.

F. VON LUSCHAN, "Die Tachtadschy und andere Ueberreste der alten Bevölkerung Lykiens" (*Archiv für Anthropologie*, vol. xix, pp. 31–53).

Page 82.

KARL PEARSON, "On the Laws of Heredity in Man" (*Biometrika*, vol. ii [1902–03], pp. 357 *et seq.*); FRANZ BOAS, "Heredity in Anthropometric Traits" (*American Anthropologist*, N. S., vol. ix [1907], pp. 453 *et seq.*).

Page 84.

1. CH. B. DAVENPORT, "Heredity of Eye-Color in Man" (*Science*, N. S., vol. xxvi [1907], pp. 589–592); "Heredity of Hair-Form in Man" (*American Naturalist*, vol. xlii, pp. 341–349).

2. G. and Ch. Davenport, "Heredity of Hair-Color in Man" (*American Naturalist*, vol. xliii, pp. 193–211).

Page 86.

Ottokar Lorenz, Lehrbuch der gesammten wissenschaftlichen Genealogie (Berlin, 1898), pp. 289 *et seq.*, 308, 310, 311.

Page 89.

W. Johannsen, Elemente der exakten Erblichkeitslehre (Jena).

Page 91.

M. D. and Raymond Pearl, "On the Relation of Race Crossing to the Sex Ratio" (*Biological Bulletin*, vol. xv [1908], pp. 194 *et seq.*).

Page 100.

1. Gustav Klemm, Allgemeine Cultur-Geschichte (Leipzig, 1843), vol. i, pp. 196 *et seq.* His opinions are accepted by A. Wuttke, Geschichte des Heidentums (Breslau, 1852–53), vol. i, p. 36.

2. Carl Gustav Carus, "Ueber die ungleiche Befahigung der verschiedenen Menschheitsstämme für höhere geistige Entwicklung" (*Denkschrift zum hundertjährigen Geburtsfeste Goethe's*, Leipzig, 1849).

3. J. A. de Gobineau, Essai sur l'inegalite des races humaines (Paris, 1853–55).

4. Nott and Gliddon, Types of Mankind (Philadelphia, 1854); Indigenous Races of the Earth (Philadelphia, 1857).

5. Theodor Waitz, Anthropologie der Naturvolker, vol. (2d ed., Leipzig, 1877).

6. Herbert Spencer, Principles of Sociology.

7. Edward B. Tylor, Researches into the Early History of Mankind; Primitive Culture.

Page 101.

Theodor Waitz, Anthropologie der Naturvolker (2d ed., 1877), vol. i, p. 387.

Pages 106, 109.

.HERBERT SPENCER, The Principles of Sociology (New York, 1893), vol. i, pp. 55 *et seq.*, 59–61.

Page 111.

G. M. SPROAT, Scenes and Studies of Savage Life (1868), p. 120.

Page 112.

1. HERBERT SPENCER, l. c., p. 70.
2. FRANZ BOAS, "The Growth of Indian Mythologies" (*Journal of American Folk-Lore*, vol. ix [1896], pp. 1–11).
3. J. MOONEY, "The Ghost-Dance Religion" (*Fourteenth Annual Report of the Bureau of Ethnology*, pp. 641 *et seq.*).

Page 113.

1. OVIEDO Y VALDES, Historia General y Natural de las Indias [1535–57] (Madrid, 1851–55), Bk. xlii, Chaps. 2, 3 (quoted from SPENCER, Descriptive Sociology, No. II, pp. 42–43).
2. RUDOLF LEHMANN, Schopenhauer.

Page 114.

G. TARDE, Les Lois de l'Imitation.

Page 116.

FRANCIS GALTON, Natural Inheritance; Hereditary Genius. KARL PEARSON, *Biometrika.*

Page 117.

1. A. WERNICH, Geographisch-medicinische Studien nach den Erlebnissen einer Reise um die Erde (Berlin, 1878), pp. 81 *et seq.*
2. RUDOLF VIRCHOW, "Die physischen Eigenschaften der Lappen" (*Verhandlungen der Berliner Gesellschaft für Anthropologie, Ethnologie u. Urgeschichte*, vol. vii [1875], pp. 34 *et seq.;* also vol. xxii [1890], p. 411).

Page 118.

1. W. H. R. RIVERS, "Observations on the Senses of the Todas" (*Journal of Psychology*, vol. i [1905], pp. 322 *et seq.*).

2. The complete results of this study have not been published. The tests on hearing were published by FRANK G. BRUNER, The Hearing of Primitive Peoples (New York, *Science Press*, 1908).

Page 120.

CHARLES DARWIN, Journal of Researches into the Natural History and Geology of the Countries visited during the Voyage of H. M. S. *Beagle* round the World (New York, 1895), pp. 228–229.

Page 121.

A brief resume of FREUD's theory will be found in the *American Journal of Psychology*, vol. xxi (1910).

Page 126.

1. For a history of these attempts, see P. TOPINARD, Éléments d'Anthropologie generale (Paris, 1885), pp. 1–147.

2. H. HUXLEY, "On the Geographical Distribution of the Chief Modifications of Mankind" (*Journal of the Ethnological Society*, N. S., vol. ii [1870], pp. 404–412).

Page 127.

FRIEDRICH MULLER, Allgemeine Ethnographie (Vienna, 1879).

Page 128.

W. Z. RIPLEY, The Races of Europe (New York, 1899); J. DENIKER, The Races of Man (London, 1900).

Page 129.

1. F. SARASIN, Ergebnisse naturwissenschaftlicher Forschungen auf Ceylon (Wiesbaden, 1892–93), vol. iii, pp. 569 *et seq.*

2. E. BALZ, "Menschenrassen Ost-Asiens mit specieller Rücksicht auf Japan" (*Verhandlungen der Berliner anthropologischen Gesellschaft*, vol. xxxiii [1901], pp. 166–189); H. TEN KATE, "Anthropologisches und Verwandtes aus Japan" (*Internationales Centralblatt für Anthropologie*, vol. vii [1902], p. 659).

3. W. JOCHELSON, The Yukaghir and the Yukaghirized Tungus (*Publications of the Jesup North Pacific Expedition*, vol. ix [1910], p. 59).

Page 131.

1. FRANZ BOAS, "A. J. Stone's Measurements of Natives of the Northwest Territories" (*Bulletin of the American Museum of Natural History*, vol. xiv [New York, 1901], pp. 53–68); "Zur Anthropologie der nordamerikanischen Indianer" (*Verhandlungen der Berliner Gesellschaft fur Anthropologie, Ethnologie und Urgeschichte*, vol. xxvii [1895], pp. 367 *et seq.*).

2. PLINY EARLE GODDARD, Life and Culture of the Hupa (*University of California Publications, American Archæology and Ethnology*, vol. i [Berkeley, 1903–04]); WASHINGTON MATTHEWS, Navaho Legends (1897); P. A. G. MORICE, "The Great Dene Race" (*Anthropos*, vols. i, ii, iv [1906, 1907, 1909]).

Page 132.

A. L. KROEBER, Types of Indian Culture in California (*University of California Publications, American Archæology and Ethnology*, vol. ii [1904–07], pp. 81–103).

Page 140.

See remarks in GEORG VON DER GABELENTZ, Die Sprachwissenschaft (Leipzig, 1891), pp. 371 *et seq.*

Page 141.

FRANZ BOAS, "On Alternating Sounds" (*American Anthropologist*, vol. ii [1889], pp. 47 *et seq.*).

Page 147.

J. W. POWELL, Introduction to the Study of Indian Languages (2d ed., Washington, Bureau of Ethnology), pp. 69 *et seq.*

Page 156.

1. E. B. TYLOR, Primitive Culture; Researches into the Early History of Mankind.

2. HERBERT SPENCER, The Principles of Sociology.

3. J. G. FRAZER, The Golden Bough; Totemism and Exogamy.

4. A. BASTIAN, Ideale Welten (Berlin, 1892); Die Welt in ihren Spiegelungen unter dem Wandel der Völkergedankens (Berlin, 1887); Allerlei aus Volks- und Menschenkunde (Berlin, 1888); Geographische und ethnologische Bilder (Jena, 1873); etc.

5. RICHARD ANDREE, Ethnographische Parallelen und Vergleiche (Stuttgart, 1878; Neue Folge, Leipzig, 1889).

6. ALBERT H. POST, Grundriss der Ethnologischen Jurisprudenz (Oldenburg and Leipzig, 1894).

Page 157.

1. RICHARD ANDREE, "Scapulimantia," in Boas Anniversary Volume (New York, G. E. Stechert, 1906), pp. 143 et seq.

2. FRANZ BOAS, Indianische Sagen von der Nord-Pacifischen Küste Amerikas (Berlin, A. Asher, 1895), pp. 338-339.

3. FRANZ HEGER, "Aderlassgerathe bei den Indianern und Papuas" (Mittheilungen der Anthropologischen Gesellschaft in Wien, vol. xxiii [1893], Sitzungsberichte, pp. 83-87).

Page 158.

ROLAND B. DIXON, "Basketry Designs of the Indians of Northern California" (Bulletin of the American Museum of Natural History, vol. xvii, p. 28).

Page 161.

1. WALDEMAR BOGORAS, The Chukchee (Publications of the Jesup North Pacific Expedition, vol. vii [Leiden, 1904-09]); FRANZ BOAS, The Central Eskimo [(Sixth Annual Report of the Bureau of Ethnology [Washington, 1888]).

2. LEONHARD SCHULTZE, Aus Namaland und Kalahari (Jena, 1907).

3. RUDOLF MARTIN. (See note 2 to p. 74.)

Page 162.

1. BOGORAS, l.c., pp. 177 et seq.; BOAS, l.c., pp. 551 et seq. (see note 1, p. 161).

2. BOAS (Ibid., p. 595).

Page **165**.

K. WEULE, Die Kultur der Kulturlosen (Stuttgart); F. RATZEL, Anthropogeographie, vol. ii (1891), p. 693.

Page **167**.

1. ED. HAHN, Die Haustiere (Leipzig, 1896), pp. 464, 465; A. DE CANDOLLE, Origin of Cultivated Plants (New York, 1886), pp. 59 *et seq.*, 139 *et seq.*

2. KARL VON DEN STEINEN, Durch Centralbrasilien (1886), pp. 310 *et seq.;* Unter den Naturvolkern Zentral-Brasiliens (1894), pp. 210–212.

3. BERTHOLD LAUFER, "The Introduction of Maize into Eastern Asia" (*Congres International des Americanistes*, xv^e Session, Quebec, 1907, vol. i, pp. 223 *et seq.*, particularly pp. 250–252). Regarding the introduction of tobacco into eastern Asia, see J. REIN, in *Petermann's Mitteilungen*, vol. xxiv (1878), pp. 215 *et seq.*

4. VICTOR HEHN, Kulturpflanzen und Haustiere (2d ed., Berlin, 1874).

Page **169**.

1. ED. HAHN, Die Entstehung der Pflugkultur (Heidelberg, 1909).

2. RICHARD LAASCH, Der Eid (Stuttgart, 1908). Laasch gives some examples of the oath in America. They are, however, remarkably few as compared to the vast material collected by him from the Old World.

Page **171**.

An exposition of BASTIAN'S point of view may be found in TH. ACHELIS, Moderne Volkerkunde (Stuttgart, 1896), pp. 189 *et seq.*

Page **173**.

1. WILHELM WUNDT, Volkerpsychologie (Leipzig, Engelmann).

2. OTTO STOLL, Suggestion und Hypnotismus in der Volkerpsychologie (Leipzig, 1894).

Page 176.

E. B. Tylor, Primitive Culture (3d ed., 1891), p. 16.

Page 177.

E. B. Tylor, "On a Method of Investigating the Development of Institutions" (*Journal of the Anthropological Institute of Great Britain and Ireland*, vol. xviii [1889], pp. 245 *et seq.*).

Page 179.

1. Otis T. Mason, The Origins of Invention (London, 1895), pp. 315 *et seq.*

2. W J McGee, "The Beginning of Zooculture" (*American Anthropologist*, vol. x [1897], pp. 215 *et seq.*).

3. Ed. Hahn, Die Haustiere und ihre Beziehungen zur Wirtschaft des Menschen; Die Entstehung der Pflugkultur (Heidelberg, 1909).

Page 180.

1. H. Colley March, in *Transactions of the Lancashire and Cheshire Antiquarian Society*, 1886, "Polynesian Ornament a Mythology" (*Journal of the Anthropological Institute of Great Britain and Ireland*, vol. xxii [1893], pp. 307 *et seq.*). Hjalmar Stolpe, "Entwicklungserscheinungen in der Ornamentik der Naturvolker" (*Mittheilungen der Anthropologischen Gesellschaft in Wien*, vol. xxii [1892], pp. 19 *et seq.*). Charles H. Read, "On the Origin and Sacred Character of Certain Ornaments of the S. E. Pacific" (*Journ. Anthr. Inst.*, vol. xxi [1892], pp. 139 *et seq.*).

2. A. C. Haddon, "The Decorative Art of British New Guinea" (*Cunningham Memoirs*, No. X [Dublin, 1894]).

3. Karl von den Steinen, Unter den Naturvolkern Zentral-Brasiliens (Berlin, 1894).

4. W. H. Holmes, "Ancient Art of the Province of Chiriqui, Colombia" (*Sixth Annual Report of the Bureau of Ethnology* [Washington, 1888], pp. 3 *et seq.*); F. W. Putnam, "Conventionalism in Ancient American Art" (*Bulletin Essex Institute*, vol. xviii [1886], pp. 155–167); George

Grant McCurdy, " The Armadillo in the Ancient Art of Chiriqui " (*Fifteenth International Congress of Americanists* [Quebec, 1907], vol. ii, pp. 147–163).

5. Von den Steinen, "Prahistorische Zeichen und Ornamente" (*Bastian Festschrift* [Berlin, 1896], pp. 247–288). The general theory of ornament has been treated from this point of view by H. Colley March, " The Meaning of Ornament, or its Archæology and its Psychology" (*Transactions of the Lancaster and Cheshire Antiquarian Society*, 1889). A. C. Haddon, Evolution in Art (1895). Ernst Grosse, Die Anfange der Kunst (1894).

Page 186.

Von den Steinen, "Die Bedeutung der Textilmuster fur den geometrischen Stil der Naturvölker" (*Correspondenz-Blatt der deutschen Gesellschaft für Anthropologie, Ethnologie und Urgeschichte*, vol. xxxv [1904], p. 126) ; Max Schmidt, Indianerstudien in Zentral-Brasilien (Berlin, 1905), pp. 330 *et seq.;* Franz Boas, "The Decorative Art of the North American Indians" (*Popular Science Monthly*, 1903, pp. 481–498) ; Heinrich Schurtz, Urgeschichte der Kultur (1900), p. 540 ; A. S. F. Hamlin, in *The American Architect and Building News* (1898).

Page 187.

1. Richard Andree, Ethnographische Parallelen und Vergleiche (Neue Folge, 1889), pp. 107 *et seq.*

2. Washington Matthews, "The Gentile System of the Navajo Indians" (*Journal of American Folk-Lore*, vol. iii [1890], pp. 89–110).

Page 188.

1. John G. Bourke, "Notes upon the Gentile Organization of the Apaches of Arizona" (*Ibid.*, pp. 111–126).

2. J. Walter Fewkes, "The Kinship of a Tanoan-speaking Community in Tusayan" (*American Anthropologist*, vol. vii [1894], pp. 162 *et seq.*).

3. FRANZ BOAS, "The Social Organization and the Secret Societies of the Kwakiutl Indians" (*Report of the U. S. National Museum for 1895* [Washington, 1897], p. 333); JOHN R. SWANTON, "Contributions to the Ethnology of the Haida" (*Publications of the Jesup North Pacific Expedition*, vol. ii [Leiden, 1905–09], pp. 102 *et seq.*).

Page 191.

A. A. GOLDENWEISER, "Totemism, an Analytical Study" (*Journal of American Folk-Lore*, vol. xxiii [1910], pp. 179 *et seq.*).

Page 192.

EDWARD WESTERMARCK, The Origin and Development of the Moral Ideas (London, 1906).

Page 194.

1. For examples see, for instance, FRANZ BOAS, Handbook of American Indian Languages (*Bulletin 40, Bureau of American Ethnology* [Washington, 1911]).

2. CARL STUMPF, Die Anfange der Musik (Leipzig, 1911).

Page 233.

CLARK WISSLER, "Decorative Art of the Sioux Indians" (*Bulletin of the American Museum of Natural History*, vol. xviii [New York, 1904], pp. 231–278).

Printed in the United States of America.

C

19978234R00164

Made in the USA
Lexington, KY
15 January 2013